GLENN COCHRANE'S
TORONTO

Published by ECW Press
2120 Queen Street East, Suite 200, Toronto, Ontario, Canada M4E 1E2

LIBRARY AND ARCHIVES CANADA CATALOGUING IN PUBLICATION

Cochrane, Glenn, 1928–
Glenn Cochrane's Toronto : Tales of the city
/ by Glenn Cochrane.

ISBN-13: 978-1-55022-712-3
ISBN-10: 1-55022-712-2

1. Toronto (Ont.)--Description and travel. I. Title.

FC3097.3.C62 2005   971.3'54105   C2005-904347-4

Editor: Joy Gugeler
Cover and Text Design: Tania Craan
Production: Mary Bowness
Cover Photo: Zoran Milich, Masterfile
Printing: Marquis Book Printing

This book is set in Adobe Garamond and Trajan

With the publication of *Glenn Cochrane's Toronto* ECW Press acknowledges the
generous financial support of the Government of Canada through the Book
Publishing Industry Development Program (BPIDP), the Canada Council for the
Arts, and the Ontario Arts Council, for our publishing activities.

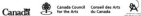

DISTRIBUTION

Canada: Jaguar Book Group, 100 Armstrong Ave., Georgetown, ON L7G 5S4

PRINTED AND BOUND IN CANADA

ECW PRESS
ecwpress.com

GLENN COCHRANE'S
TORONTO

Tales of the City

ECW PRESS

In memory of
Ralph Gordon Cochrane

CONTENTS

Late Toronto mayor Phil Givens in The Archer's crosshairs.

THE CAMERA IS ROLLING

Preface

On January 15, 1993, I retired after 25 years as a reporter at CFTO-TV, and what a quarter century it was. Five times a week on the 6:00 p.m. WorldBeat News and again on the 11:30 NightBeat News I interviewed politicians, beauty queens, hockey heroes, and hundreds of ordinary Canadians with great stories to tell. Wayne Gretzky, Mike Myers, Carol Channing, George Burns, Liberace, and Honest Ed Mirvish feature prominently, and you will meet them all later — but first a little more about me.

I was born in Hamilton, Ontario in 1928 and grew up in the west end in the foothills of Hamilton "Mountain," an exaggeration that is a stubborn matter of civic pride precisely because it seems to upset the transplanted Westerners in our midst. My father was a linotype operator and part-time sportswriter while my mother raised Marjorie, Paul, Gord, and me in a remarkably harmonious household considering it had six inhabitants and only one bathroom.

I worked in sales after leaving high school, and although the money was good, I wanted more. I went to the *Hamilton Spectator* and asked the personnel manager if there was an opening in the crossword puzzle department as I was pretty good at solving them. There wasn't, but he did introduce me to city editor Deny Harvey who told me that if I was really interested in the news business he would give me a series of evening assignments. I didn't get paid and I had to cover all my expenses, but for the next few weeks I willingly covered church suppers to prove my worth. Eventually I was hired to do general assignment stories, obituaries, court reporting, lost dogs, golden wedding anniversaries, and finally the crime beat — you get the picture. I went on to the Maclean publishing empire in Toronto and Broadcast News before joining CFTO.

In 1958 John Bassett and others purchased a 20-acre parcel of land in Scarborough for $132,084. Bassett was publisher of the *Toronto Telegram* and part of a coalition formed to apply for a license to operate a TV station in Toronto, which then had a population of about 672,400. The group was bankrolled by John David Eaton, of the Eaton merchandising empire, and other prominent players such as Joel Aldred, a nationally known radio and television announcer, and Ted Rogers, son of the founder of powerful Toronto radio station CFRB.

Two years after the land purchase, the Board of Broadcast Governors (BBG), a regulatory body established by the Conservative government of John Diefenbaker, met in Toronto to consider nine applicants for a prize described by media mogul Lord Thomson of Fleet as "A license to print your own money." The hearing began in the Oak Room at Union Station on March 17, 1960, better remembered by some as the date of one of the biggest snowfalls in Toronto's history. The storm may have caused the power failure that suddenly darkened the room just as the Baton-Aldred-Rogers team, led by John Bassett, was starting its pitch with a closed-circuit presentation of news, entertainment, and sports. The blackout lasted five minutes, but unperturbed by the unexpected development, Bassett ad libbed a performance that impressed even the competition. Shortly after the hearing concluded the BBG recommended that the Bassett group be granted the licence, and on New Year's Day 1961, CFTO-TV, Toronto's first independent television station, went on the air at 9:45 p.m. with a pre-taped show of CFTO's official opening on December 19.

The ceremonial ribbon cutting was performed by Lieutenant-Governor Keiller Mackay, and as soon as the formalities concluded the fledgling station opened with a telethon for Community Living Ontario. The event raised $210,000. Company executives considered it a highly successful launch; however, this view was not shared by two of the city's daily newspapers. The *Globe and Mail* arts and entertainment critic dwelt at length on the technical difficulties encountered by the CFTO production team and summarized his opening-night impressions by comparing it to a block party located in the middle of an icefield. The lead story on page one of the *Globe and Mail* of January 2 instead covered the death of a 10-year-old girl who died in a fire at a cottage on Ward's Island, a blizzard in Montreal, the war in Vietnam, and the New Year's baby born at one second past midnight in the Salvation Army Grace Hospital. CFTO fared no better in the *Toronto Star*. Their story also focused on the station's first-night glitches and dismissed the entire telethon performance with the withering phrase "Dreary and inept television."

When CFTO first went on the air, its 925-foot transmission tower immediately became Scarborough's best-known landmark. Apple orchards still flourished on farmland bordering CFTO on McCowan Avenue almost as far north as Steeles Avenue, and the road to the station was a tree-lined country lane complete with the odd rabbit burrow.

The early evening WorldBeat newscast built a solid
base of viewers, and plans were well underway in early
1968 to launch a half-hour newscast called NightBeat
News with anchorman Joe Mariash, weatherman Dave
Devall, and gravel-voiced sports director Pat Marsden and
his sidekick Fergie Oliver. A 30-minute newscast may
now seem typical, but until then the station's late-night
news had been a "rip-and-read" operation — the station
announcer would rip off the latest summary from the
Canadian Press newswire service and read it over the air.
Add a few items from the police blotter, throw in a
weather report and the sports scores, and, for a small
expenditure of time and money, you had a local newscast.

Local TV critics wondered just how NightBeat
would do against the mighty CBC's well-established
niche in the market, but Mariash's distinctive manner
on the anchor desk, Devall's entertaining delivery, and
Marsden's opinionated viewpoints soon built up a sizeable following. I had known Joe Mariash when I
worked at the *Hamilton Spectator* and he was a reporter
with a local radio station. We shared many a pint at the
Hamilton Press Club, a friendship that got me an interview with news director Ted Stuebing when NightBeat
was starting up. Ted seemed more impressed with the
fact we both came from Hamilton than he was with my
curriculum vitae, but I got a call to start as a writer two
weeks later. I also wrote copy for the WorldBeat dinner
hour newscast anchored by Ken Cavanagh. He liked to

finish the newscast with a "kicker" or "closer," a humorous or offbeat item, so, amid the daily deluge of bad news, it was my task to cull a few sentences concerning matters of a lighter nature.

The day I got my big break the day news manager, Jim Bard, suggested I take a cameraman and cover a story for the newscast closer because all the reporters were busy. It was well received by my superiors, so, while I continued my desk duties, I was occasionally sent to cover events of a peculiar nature along the lines of "Jersey cow gives birth to two-headed alligator." Eventually I was told to produce one of these stories every Friday. (In those days CFTO News only operated from Monday to Friday.) The anchor would introduce my segment and then say, "And with that story, here is Our Man Friday, Glenn Cochrane." That tag line, and my graphic over the anchor's shoulder, established me with the viewing audience.

One night I was invited to talk about my work-related experiences to a church group. We all enjoyed a nice meal and as soon as the dessert bowls had been cleared away a pleasant woman stood up and began to introduce me to the audience. She said some flattering things about me and concluded with the words, "And now it is my pleasure to introduce the man who sends me to bed every Friday evening with a smile on my face." A dead silence ensued, broken finally by a man who cried out, "What about your husband?"

A few months after that incident I was made assignment editor, sending the reporting teams to cover the day's stories. The assignment desk operated out of the Telegram building on Front Street just west of Spadina Avenue, rather than in the Scarborough headquarters, because the downtown location was closer to news-generating sources such as Queen's Park, City Hall, police headquarters, and of course Maple Leaf Gardens. The stories were shot on film, brought back to the Tely building, and then forwarded from there to the studios in Agincourt for processing and editing. That meant sending a car to navigate the Don Valley at rush hour, but fortunately an unflappable CFTO driver named Jimmie Downer always got it to the station on time. Later, in a move I like to believe was fuelled by public demand, I was excused from my assignment desk duties and instructed to spin human interest reports five nights a week.

Toronto was feeling pretty good about itself in those days. There was work to be had in all occupations, particularly in construction south of Queen Street between Church Street and University Avenue, and north on University to Gerrard Street. The new City Hall opened in 1964, attracting attention internationally, and Nathan Phillips Square became the city's unofficial gathering place. One of its most popular features is the Henry Moore sculpture titled the Archer, which is situated just west of the main entrance. It is the legacy of the late

Phil Givens who, when he was mayor, bought it with $50,000 raised by public donations. A considerable percentage of the electorate was nonetheless convinced the work was purchased with taxpayer's money, an issue that cost Givens the 1966 election. He has always maintained he was defeated by the Archer and not by the quality of the opposition. This makes him, by his own assessement, the only Toronto politician who lost an lost an election to a sculpture. However, Givens' enthusiasm for the work *is* widely thought to be responsible for Moore's commitment to Toronto, evidenced by a major collection at the Art Gallery of Ontario.

Fifty thousand dollars for a Henry Moore work would seem like a bargain today, but a good wage was $150 a week then — that bought a men's wrinkle-shy tropical blend suit for a mere $39.98 including a vest and a spare pair of trousers. Loblaws was offering eight cans of Heinz baby food for 99 cents, Honest Ed's Door Crasher specials featured a 47-ounce container of Saniflush for 25 cents, and a fellow could drive away from the automobile dealer's showroom with a brand new Dodge Dart for $2270 without GST or PST.

The fact that the Maple Leafs defeated the Montreal Canadiens by a score of 3–1 on May 2, 1967 to win the Stanley Cup for the 11th time only added to the buoyant mood in the city. The clinching goal was scored at the 19:13 mark of the third period by George Armstrong and that triggered a city-wide celebration that was not equalled until the Blue Jays won their first World Series in 1992.

Fortune magazine called Toronto "the world's newest great city," *Harper's* described it as "a model of the alternative future," and the late actor Peter Ustinov famously said that, "Toronto is New York run by the Swiss." When Jane Jacobs moved to Toronto from New York City in 1969, she told a local newspaper reporter that, "Toronto is the most hopeful and healthy city in North America," but she added this waring: "Few of us profit from the mistakes of others and perhaps Toronto will prove to share this disability. If so, I am at least grateful to enjoy this great city before its destruction."

While writing about my experiences during that quarter century, I fell in love with that cantankerous, bountiful patchwork of a city called Toronto all over again. It was a great city then and it is a great city today; economic charts take the temperature of a city, they can't measure its heartbeat.

Al Schoenborn.

Fancy footwork is required during the annual floods on the Toronto Islands (Manitou Hotel, 1952).

BIG DEEDS AND WATER FIGHTS

Little Italy and the Islands

In the early 1960s 12 per cent of Toronto's population was of Italian origin, and another 9 per cent came from Poland, Russia, and Ukraine. Attracted by affordable housing and the prospect of jobs in the many industries in the area, large numbers of immigrants settled in the city's west end, and by the late 1960s streets like Ossington Avenue were an eclectic mix of the old and the new. Families with the surnames Iozzo, Kuzniak, and Prakopyshyn were neighbours to earlier arrivals named

Bryson, MacDougall, and Reid. Goldstein Dry Goods and Gus Longo Fruits were just a few blocks from the Russian Culture Club, the Lithuanian Hall, and Branch 346 of the Polish War Vets.

The newcomers brightened up drab streets by planting flower beds and building pergolas for their grapes; they brought music and a sense of style that was new to their new city. In short, they brought *brio*. The heart of Little Italy, College Street between Bathurst and Ossington Avenues, featured clothing stores, outdoor fruit markets, cafés, restaurants, and European fare that added up to a distinctive and beguiling experience.

The young Italians who settled in the area worked as roofers, carpenters, and labourers, struggling up to the back doors of houses with bags of coal in the winter and huge blocks of ice in the summer. Aurelio Galipo and his brothers Frank and Joe came to Toronto in 1950 sponsored by an uncle. They spoke no English. Shortly after their arrival Aurelio tucked an English-language dictionary in his pocket and headed for the Rosedale subway station, which was still under construction. His uncle had underlined the word "work" in the dictionary so Aurelio met the foreman, pointed to it, and was taken on at $1.15 an hour.

But the Galipo brothers had bigger ideas. In 1959 they started the Sicilian Ice Cream Café on College Street, three blocks west of Grace Street. The venture

Ice cream made while you wait (mixing machines in the back room).

Uncle Joe (Guiseppe) Galipo keeps it all in the family as he serves a cuppa joe to his brother Frank (Francesco, far right) and customers at the Sicilian Ice Cream Café.

was an immediate success. The brothers worked 16 hours a day, seven days a week mixing ice cream in a garage at the back of their property. In addition to the ten flavours on the menu they also provided fresh cups of cappuccino and espresso, which proved an instant sensation.

Aurelio truly believed in the superiority of their ice cream and is still a passionate promoter of the café's tasty offerings. Brother Joe later went on to a highly successful sales career in the brewing industry. Brother Frank, who had lost his right arm, was rumoured to have sacrificed the limb in a dispute involving the Mafia. The sad truth is that it happened in 1943 when allied planes bombed the town of Capo D'Orlando in Sicily where the Galipo family lived. Their father was killed in that same raid.

When the brothers arrived, College Street was solidly established as the heart of Toronto's Italian population and a growing number of businesses catered to the community. Campo Brothers Dry Goods had shelves full of needles and thread and the brightly coloured yarn that young mothers needed for their family's clothing. The Sicilia Bakery and Pastries produced a steady supply of amaretti, biscotti, and candied fruits. A huge laundry on Crawford Street did a roaring business because nobody had a washing machine in those days.

A soccer field at College and Shaw Streets was one

of the few recreational facilities available to youth in the neighbourhood. With nowhere else to go, young men gathered at street corners, and police officers on foot patrol were constantly telling them to move along. A young officer named Julian Fantino almost single-handedly defused the situation by telling his superiors that the police were acting unfairly; eventually the force adopted friendlier tactics. Fantino eventually became Toronto's chief of police and retired in 2005.

Every working man's district requires a neighbour-hood pub and the Monarch Tavern, on the corner of Clinton and Henderson Streets on Little Italy's eastern flank, served that purpose for many years. From the outside it looked like any Canadian beer parlour, but the Monarch was a little different. Its decor was the result of a renovation made necessary when an irate husband threw a handmade bomb at a man he suspected of working the swing shift with his wife while he himself was working the night shift at a factory.

The Monarch filled with loyal customers from all over Toronto every weekday noon hour. I decided to interview some of them about the rising price of coffee due to an infestation that had done extensive damage to the coffee bean crop in Brazil. People expressed fear that the price of a cup of coffee in Toronto could exceed the price of a glass of beer, so I asked the patrons if they thought coffee breaks would be replaced by beer breaks. The first people I asked declined to be interviewed because they owned businesses and thought it would be bad form if their employees watched the news that night and saw their bosses having lunch in a beer parlour. One man would not go on camera because he was a Provincial Court judge. Even the table of well-dressed gents proved to be undercover cops and gave me the boot.

During the 1970s and 1980s that room was ruled by Peter Pesce, whom generations of admirers will remember as one of the most unusual waiters in the history of Toronto. Among his many talents Peter was a master of the ignore — you could never seem to catch his eye. He'd be slinging beer on the far side of the room when he'd suddenly head straight for your table before veering off to serve the people at the table beside you. To make matters worse, those other people had just come in. No amount of arm flailing would do the trick until he tired of his game. When your beer did arrive the first round was always on the house; the long delay was all in fun.

Sometimes Peter would bring a jewel box over to a table and ask some unwitting soul if the necklace it contained was made of real pearls. "Take a good look," Peter would command, and when the victim leaned in for a closer examination, Peter would press a hidden trigger and catch him right in the eye with a stream of water. At least I think it was water; with Peter you never knew. On those rare occasions when things got too quiet for his liking he would yell "Last call!" and rush around the room snatching up beer glasses with scarcely a sip taken from them, all the while commanding us to leave the place immediately. At other times he would stage fire drills causing the quiet streets around the hotel to suddenly fill with laughing men who milled about before obediently returning to their tables once Peter gave the all clear.

In the late 1970s one of the U.S. networks had a popular show called *Real People*, a precursor to the reality TV shows of today. As the name suggests, it was all about real people doing real things. One day a crew showed up to film Peter's antics. He was in top form until it came time for him to make a one-sentence statement into the camera. The producers had done their research for the segment thoroughly, but they didn't know that Peter was incapable of saying even the shortest of sentences without swearing. Witnesses said it took 25 takes before the crew got the sanitized clip they wanted. *Real People* went off the air shortly after and there are Monarch patrons who believe to this day that the show blew its budget trying to get Peter to clean up his vocabulary.

Not everybody loved Peter. One day another waiter named Percy approached my table, and leaning into my ear, he delivered a tirade against Peter's 10-year routine. "He never changes his act," Percy complained, "and if he doesn't do something about it soon I'm going to kill him." Peter never did alter his act, if he had his adoring fans would have revolted. He's gone now and the Monarch has morphed into a martini lounge. Wherever he is, I hope he doesn't know that.

Another local hero came to Little Italy with her family in 1905 and a few years later married a community activist named Joseph Bagnato. Grace Bagnato gave birth to 13 children yet somehow found the time and energy to learn to speak Yiddish, Polish, and Ukrainian to communicate with her neighbours in Little Italy's cosmopolitan community. She became the first Italian-Canadian woman to serve as a court interpreter in the Ontario judicial system. When she died in 1950 at the age of 59 a grateful neighbourhood erected a plaque in her memory at the corner of Grace and Mansfield Streets.

The plaque is in a small park just across the street from the Church of St. Francis. The church was built in 1903 and for over a century it has served as a place of worship, a venue for all rites of passage, and a refuge for the weary at heart. But every December for over 30 years St. Francis has shed its workaday image and presented a spectacle that has earned it recognition well beyond its parish boundaries.

It all began in 1971 when Father Arthur Lattanzi decided it would be a good idea to put up a nativity tableau at Christmas near the front door of the church. It began simply with Mary and Joseph and the infant Jesus in the manger. Over the years that humble scene

BIG DEEDS AND WATER FIGHTS

took on a life of its own and now includes a backdrop of at least 50 evergreen trees, a chorus of choirboys, a flock of sheep, a couple of donkeys, and three wise men bearing gifts sitting astride camels. The scene is warmly traditional, except that it also includes a thoroughly modern filly with flowing mane and the regal bearing of a thoroughbred. Herein lies the merchandising genius of Father Lattanzi. He pointed out that every nativity scene had sheep, camels, and donkeys, but none of them had a horse. "That horse will get people talking," he said, "and they will always remember what the Church of St. Francis has accomplished." History has proven him right. A parishioner named Pasquale Martino has been in charge of assembling this huge entourage and even though he and his crew have all passed the 80-year mark, they show no signs of relinquishing their duties.

Nearby, on a bustling stretch of College Street between Clinton and Grace, the street signs all read Johnny Lombardi Way. In an area where older structures are the norm, the modern CHIN International Radio building sticks out like a beacon. When it opened in 1982 it served as a triumphant exclamation mark to a life that began December 4, 1915 when Lombardi was born on the kitchen table of a tenement house in downtown Toronto.

One of his first full-time jobs was back-page editor of an Italian weekly newspaper where he wrote a column titled "The Snipper Snooper." But music was his real interest and eventually The Johnny Lombardi Orchestra, with Johnny on the trumpet, was playing engagements all over Toronto. After wartime service with the Canadian Army in England, France, Belgium, Holland, and Germany he returned to Canada in 1946 and opened a grocery store on College Street in Little Italy. To draw attention to his young business he began producing radio programs emphasizing music and news from Italy. On June 6, 1966, CHIN Radio International went on the air broadcasting from facilities on the second floor of the family supermarket.

Johnny Lombardi thought along the same lines as David Crombie, Toronto's mayor in the 1970s, who fought pressure from developers to demolish single-family dwellings and erect high-rises in old neighbourhoods. Much of Toronto's downtown core was demolished during the building frenzy of the 1960s and 1970s, until Crombie halted the destruction by imposing the "45-foot bylaw," a 45-foot height limit on new buildings that had no legal force but was designed to keep skyscrapers at bay.

Years later the Scottish Crombie told me he chose four and five because they were the last two digits in the date (1745) of the Battle of Culloden in which the Scots fought the British army. Crombie believed that commerce depended on investment, investment depended on stability, stability flowed from neighbourhoods, and

Johnny Lombardi's statue points to the heart of Little Italy at the intersection of Grace and College Streets.

neighbourhoods were a collective of families and homes. Lombardi helped to turn Little Italy into a vibrant part of Toronto.

The intersection of Grace and College Streets is Little Italy's spiritual crossroads, and a fitting location for Piazza Johnny Lombardi — a dedication to the memory of the area's most beloved son. I interviewed Francine Frimeth, who had been Johnny's secretary from 1976 until she retired in 2000, after the dedication ceremony. She remembered the time Johnny phoned her the morning one of her relatives died and offered her money for funeral expenses.

A granite bench boasts a bronze figure of a smiling

Lombardi with one arm extended in a welcoming gesture towards a small boy. I like to think the boy is listening as Lombardi tells him the story of his life. Although Lombardi received many honours and awards it wasn't his style to work those details into a conversation.

Part of Johnny Lombardi's legacy was the CHIN Picnic, held on Centre Island. Like Little Italy, the three Toronto Islands constitute a distinctive community with a clear sense of indentity. Records dating back to the early 1800s indicate that First Nations people lived on the islands, which were then a peninsula connected to the mainland. A violent storm in 1858 severed the neck of the peninsula and created a five-foot-deep channel wide enough for ship traffic.

During the Depression of the 1930s needy families lived in jerry-built houses on the Islands, and after 1945 many World War II veterans, unable to settle in the city due to a severe post-war housing shortage, moved there with their young families. The population fluctuated considerably over the years, but a census taken in 2003 established that 650 people live in 262 houses on Ward's Island and Algonquin Island, both of which are located in the east end of the land mass. The other principal space, Centre Island, lies near the Island Airport and is used for recreational purposes.

People have been living on the Islands for over 200 years, but, for the last fifty years the powers that be have being trying to get them to leave. The rumblings began in earnest in 1953 with the formation of the Metropolitan Toronto Council, a body made up of elected representatives from the City of Toronto and the suburbs.

The first Metro Parks Commissioner was Tommy Thompson, a personable and influential man who was determined to remove all residential development from the Island and turn the area into a huge park. Leases were terminated, Metro work crews bulldozed and burned vacant buildings, and eviction dates were issued and then changed. Residents were not allowed to make repairs to their homes, and inspectors were stationed on the Island ferries with instructions to apprehend anyone trying to smuggle building materials into the area. This didn't entirely stop the flow of illicit two-by-fours or cement bags thanks to resourceful Islanders. One man built a raft and floated supplies across the bay under cover of darkness, and Island archivist Alfred Fulton reports that more than one baby buggy was wheeled off a ferry with contraband cement blocks or other building materials concealed beneath its tiny passenger.

However, the uncertainty of the situation caused many families to flee the Island, leaving unwanted furniture on offer in a communal pile. This proved to be a bonanza for a book editor named Olive Koyama. She used to summer on the Island and one year she salvaged enough discarded furniture to fully equip her apartment when she returned to the city in the autumn. Despite the problems, residents soldiered on, come hell or high water, to employ one of their favourite sayings, and there was certainly enough of the latter. There are few if any full basements in the houses because the water level is so high that residents of Ward Island, called "Wardies," facetiously refer to their next-door land mass as Algonquin Heights because the land there is six inches higher.

This ingenuity, community spirit, and sense of identity made the islands the perfect spot for the CHIN picnic, which was held on Centre Island for the first time in 1966. Initially the picnic was a showcase for international stars like Hong Kong's Johnny Yip, singer-songwriter Gianluca Grignani from Italy, or Paco Bandeira from Portugal, and for wonderful Italian food — including the spaghetti dig-in, where competitors slurped their way through mounds of pasta in a race to see who could eat the most in the least amount of time. Lombardi soon reasoned that the picnic could not exist on spaghetti-eating contests alone, so he introduced the Miss CHIN Bikini Contest. It should be noted here that there is also a Mr. CHIN Bikini competition, but somehow it has never excited the same enthusiasm.

The annual bikini contest was delayed on July 7, 1974 when Prime Minister Pierre Trudeau paid a pre-election visit to the picnic with his wife Margaret. It was a shrewd piece of political timing because the federal

Contestants are determined to put their best face forward at the annual CHIN Picnic spaghetti dig-in.

election was to be held the next day and an estimated 100,000 people jammed onto Centre Island to meet Canada's version of royalty.

The first time I covered the contest, my cameraman and I were assigned a place on a picnic table right beside the runway. The picnic drew crowds of about 25,000 at the time and I believe most of them were on that table. While I had no trouble relating to their interest in the goings on, I resented the fact that they were blocking my cameraman's view. When I asked them kindly to step aside on the grounds that we were working media, an assortment of grandmothers, seven-foot basketball players, and muscular construction workers assured me that they, too, were part of the working media. When I pressed them for proof of this, they waved still cameras in my general direction and explained they had been hired to take pictures for the radio station.

The cameraman and I were unable to counter this unassailable logic with arguments of our own, but I can tell you that what with the sun beating down on our un-protected heads and the difficulty of maintaining our footing on the overcrowded table, it was no picnic cover-ing that picnic! I eventually was rewarded for the hardships I encountered in the early days; I was appointed a contest judge. I was given a comfortable chair located on a shady part of the stage within easy view of the contestants. When the judging was finished, and it seemed to me to be over in a matter of seconds,

A candidate in the Miss CHIN bikini contest struts her stuff on a makeshift runway fashioned from picnic tables.

Lombardi presented me with a beer as a token of his thanks.

Lombardi's picnic led the way for other festivities that graced Centre Island. In 1967 the Island hosted Toronto's West Indian community, who staged a Trinidad-style "jump up" and that first Caribana became an annual event. One year later the Mariposa Festival set up stages on the Island and featured stars Joni Mitchell and Murray McLaughlin. In 1972, Bob Dylan created a near riot when he appeared unexpectedly. These events and the picnic itself attracted a considerable crowd; in fact, so many flocked to the little island that the picnic eventually outgrew its first home and moved to the Exhibition grounds.

Caribana celebrations were in full swing by 1971.

The Prince's Gates have offered a royal welcome to Ex visitors for more than half a century.

COTTON CANDY AND OLD BATTLES

Lower Bathurst

The annual Canadian National Exhibition, the "Ex," has long been associated with impressive displays of pageantry, but there was an extra snap to the ceremonies on August 30, 1927. That is when the impressive eastern entrance to the grounds was officially opened by Edward, Prince of Wales, and Prince George (the future King George vi). In their honour the structure was called the Princes' Gates. That title caused many misunderstandings whenever I reported from that location. It didn't matter how carefully I pronounced "Princes' Gates," there were always viewers who called protesting that I had said "Princess Gates." To avoid the hassle, I began reporting from the Dufferin Gates instead. The royals would have saved me a lot of grief if they had been dukes when they officiated.

The Ex has changed dramatically since the Industrial Exhibition Association held its first annual trade fair there in 1879. In the interim, the emphasis has moved from heavy machinery demonstrations to heavy metal bands and other expressions of popular entertainment. In 1883 the Scenic Auto-Dip, an early roller coaster, scared the wits out of those foolhardy souls brave enough to try it, and the evening show featured the Daughters of Canada singing "The Maple Leaf Forever." Old-time fiddling contests drew large audiences, and lectures entitled "Does a Tea Room Pay? Yes" drew avid audiences.

Less than 75 years later, in 1955, the grandstand show featured attractions including Ed Sullivan, the Four Lads, Lake Ontario swimmer Marilyn Bell, and a Mountie chorus. As the Ex grew older it kept growing younger in its approach to providing fair-goers with the latest diversions and innovations available. In fact, the only thing that hasn't changed is the demand from some quarters that it be done away with.

CNE lover David Garrick, a past general manager of the Ex, had much to do with making sure that didn't

Lake Ontario conqueror Marilyn Bell prefers dry land for this 1955 photo with CNE boss Jack Arthur.

happen, and now, 125 years strong, the CNE still stands as a favourite summer diversion. Garrick has held many high-profile positions in Toronto over the years: President of the CN Tower, Vice-President of Corporate Affairs for the SkyDome, CEO of the Royal Agricultural Winter Fair, and Chairman of the Grey Cup Festival. In short, he is the type of manager who would build an ark if deluged — and that's exactly what he did when he was running the 1981 fair. It rained for 14 consecutive days that year, setting a sodden record that remains unchallenged. The only thing that fell faster than the raindrops was the attendance at the fair. Faced with the possibility of a huge operating deficit, Garrick commanded the CNE works department to build an ark, five feet high and 14 feet long. He then filled it with hundreds of toy animals and the hastily-built float with its pint-sized passengers was ready in time for the wind-up Labour Day festivities. Despite his last-minute heroics, the Ex lost almost two million dollars that year, but he will be remembered for the way he floated an ark instead of a loan.

Later Garrick showed he could save the Ex's money as well as spend it. One year the famous Alpine Ride broke down, stranding dozens of passengers for six hours. To compensate them for their ordeal, Garrick presented them all with lifetime passes on the popular attraction. Unfortunately the ride was demolished not long after his generous gesture.

All aboard the ark! Audiences rose to the occasion during the soaking wet 1981 Ex.

One of the Ex's popular features was a cooking show starring Etta Sawyer, an expert chef who operated a successful cooking school on Yonge Street. For several years she invited me to demonstrate the preparation of my version of meatball soup, and with her help the show went along quite professionally except for one unfortunate incident in which a large piece of plastic somehow wound up in the cooking pot. I assisted as well in the judging of various homemade delicacies including jams, jellies, and bread.

I also helped judge the Miss Queen of the Fair contest, featuring young women from rural communities attesting that their hometown was the friendliest place in Ontario. One woman, her face aglow with sincerity, recounted a story of a flat tire on a rural side road one rainy night. "I was standing by the car wondering how I could fix the mess," she said, "but within a few minutes three or four cars stopped and the drivers volunteered their assistance." As a man who's had such an experience, I can tell you that help was not so quickly forthcoming in my case. I'd be standing there to this day if I'd relied on handsome gentlemen to come to my aid.

In its heyday in the 1970s, three million people visited the Ex every year. I have always loved the Ex, which is a good thing, because for 25 years, every summer, I was expected to do a daily story on it for CFTO. But even with all my enthusiasm, over the course of a quarter century, creativity can run a little dry. I will always

Seasoned chef Etta Sawyer and I have a stirring discussion at the A&P Kitchen Theatre.

appreciate the help I got from Garrick and publicity director Howard Tate.

Garrick and Tate made sure I had access to celebrities like Ed Sullivan, Frank Sinatra, and Bob Hope, not to mention Evel Knievel, who brought his supercharged motorcycle act to the Ex one year. He wore heavy rings and a somewhat glazed expression, but I suppose it is only reasonable to assume that if you are going to make a living vaulting your motorcycle over 18 Mack trucks then you probably require more than a little supercharging yourself.

I also encountered Diane Dupuy, founder of Famous

Daredevil Evel Knievel pulls a wheelie before an Ex-pectant crowd.

Ed Sullivan discusses dance routines with the Canadettes before his "really big shoo" at the 1955 Ex.

PEOPLE Players, whose internationally renowned black light theatre company of mentally challenged young people offers hour-long live performances that combine music, dance, and dazzling special effects with life-sized characters that pay tribute to the music and artistry of a host of celebrity singers and actors. Dupuy was given her first break by Garrick when he found a small performing space for her troupe at the Ex. Diane invited me to do a striptease during one of the performances. This spectacle pales in comparison to the Scottish bandsmen in the Bavarian Beer Garden who worked their way through 120 kegs of beer before performing that evening in the Scottish World festival. It is true they were small kegs, but still . . .

During my years at CFTO I worked with many talented camerapersons who provided input that made me look better than if I had been left to my own devices. One July day I was with cameraman Tom Johnston doing a "stand-up" on a busy stretch of Bloor Street West. I had just finished when a stranger walking by stuck his face into the microphone and said in a loud, clear voice, "That was terrible." It was all said in fun, I think, and after some good-natured joshing the stranger went on his way and I signalled Tom that I wanted to do another sign-off minus that bit of improv street theatre. Tom thought the line funny and persuaded me to leave it in. It was so well received on that evening's newscast that I began to occasionally ask passersby to deliver that remark right after I said, "Glenn Cochrane reporting." I dropped it from my repertoire when I realized I never had any trouble finding strangers willing to go on camera and convincingly declare that my report was terrible.

One of my most memorable Ex reports was born of a second instance of collaboration with my cameraman — and of desperation. In the absence of a better idea, I suggested we shoot a story from a child's perspective. Tom Ruppel, my cameraman, spent the next few hours walking around the hot Ex grounds with the camera dangling from the end of his arm while I scuttled beside him in a half-crouch. I learned that you have to put up with a lot when you're trying to fight your way through a forest of adult legs and suffer the ever-present danger of being squashed and dripped on by ice cream. Not to mention the fact that you can never find your mother when you need her.

One Labour Day, I covered a spelling bee for 10 year olds but by some weird coincidence all of the finalists spoke in very soft voices making it difficult for the camera to pick up their answers as they carefully enunciated their way through "sycophant" or "amalgamation." To make matters worse the Air Show was on and every time the contest reached a critical juncture, a squadron of jets roared overhead drowning out the contestants' replies. All of this commotion forced the assorted proud relatives in the audience to lean forward in their chairs to better hear what was happening on stage. Occasionally one would loose his balance and crash to the ground thus causing the entire audience to rush to his assistance, abandoning the scared but determined contestant they had come to support.

In 1989 my cameraman's two-way radio crackled with the news that a Snow Bird had gone down in Lake Ontario not far from where we were standing. We moved quickly enough to get footage of the rescue attempt before we were kicked off the site. The aircraft was piloted by Captain Shane Antaya, who died in the crash.

One of Toronto's most enduring rumours is the one predicting that the CNE's unique old buildings will be demolished to make way for condominiums, or estate homes for the ultra-rich, or an industrial park, but somehow these grandiose plans never succeed in getting off the ground. One victory was secured when public opinion saved a building considered by many to be Toronto's most important military installation. In the 1830s, America's hopes of wresting Canada away from Great Britain were still strong despite the outcome of the War of 1812, and when construction began on forts in Detroit and Buffalo, the British thought it prudent to counter with measures of their own. In 1841, to strengthen the defenses at Toronto, seven stone buildings were constructed on the site of what is now Exhibition Place. This was named the New Fort to distinguish it from the Old Fort York at Bathurst Street.

The New Fort became redundant as relations between Canada and the U.S. improved, and gradually the seven buildings fell into a state of disuse.

During World War II, part of the complex was converted to emergency housing, but when the city assumed control of the buildings in 1947 nobody knew what to do with them. Some were demolished, and eventually the decision was made to save only the officers' quarters. The surviving structure is located west of the Princes' Gates, and was named the Stanley Barracks in honour of the former Governor General Lord Stanley, perhaps better known as the man who donated that emblem of NHL supremacy, the Stanley Cup.

In 1927 and again in 1932, the CNE proposed demolishing the Barracks to improve the eastern entrance and allow extension of the midway, but the idea was quietly dropped. In 1953 the Ex again revived its proposal. A huge public outcry prompted Ex officials to hastily back down and the future existence of the venerable building was assured in 1959 when it was officially designated the Marine Museum of Upper Canada by Lord Louis Mountbatten, then admiral of the NATO fleet.

The Barracks operated as a museum, but it has also served other purposes over the years. There was a charming restaurant on the ground floor, its lovely old rooms the scene of many evening functions. After many years of negotiating, the contents of the museum were moved on July 1, 1998 to a new site at Pier 4, next to the

Harbourfront Centre. It is a much more accessible site than the more isolated location on the Ex grounds, but local historians fear that in the future the Stanley Barracks will be demolished and the Ex will get the parking space it has long coveted. The pros and cons of the move will be a cause of debate for many years, but perhaps the definitive word on the subject should be left to the late J.A. McGinnis who was managing director of the Toronto Historical Board in the 1970s. When informed that civic leaders had taken a strong interest in moving Stanley Barracks to a lakefront location, Brigadier McGinnis had this to say: "It's none of their bloody business. Historic sites should be left alone."

Generations of Toronto residents have benefited because historic sites *have* been left alone, chief among them that Old Fort referred to earlier, Fort York. In 1793 the Lieutenant-Governor of Upper Canada, John Graves Simcoe, ordered the construction of a garrison near Front and Bathurst Streets. The threat of war with the United States was real, so he wanted to establish a naval base that would give him control of Lake Ontario. The garrison was called Fort York and the British Army stationed soldiers there from 1793 to 1870.

Fortunately Canada's relations with the U.S. have stabilized considerably over the years, and today Fort York is operated as a historic site by the City of Toronto through the Toronto Historical Board. It is Canada's largest collection of War of 1812 buildings.

Re-enactments of old battles complete with musket fire and dramatic collapses on the field of battle are a well-attended tourist attraction today, but there was a time when the garrison rang with the sounds of real gunfire and the cries of wounded soldiers were genuine.

On April 27, 1813 American warships sailed up Lake Ontario past the Scarborough Bluffs on their way to a landing point between Dufferin Street and Roncesvalles Avenue in what today is Parkdale. A force of 1,750 commanded by Brigadier General Zebulon Pike made its way to shore and began battling east toward Fort York. The outnumbered defenders, consisting mainly of British troops and Mississauga and Ojibway warriors, could not stem the enemy tide, and when they were pushed back to Fort York, officers sounded the order to withdraw. Before retreating, the British blew up the powder magazine and 250 American troops were killed or wounded. One of those killed was Brigadier General Pike, after whom Pike's Peak in Colorado is named. The officer was struck by debris as he stood near the present site of the Princes' Gates.

The Garrison Burying Ground, the first cemetery in the Town of York, was established by the British Army as the final resting place for soldiers killed in the War of 1812, and for their families. The last known burial took place in 1863 when Private James McQuarrick was interred. The ground is an inviting expanse of land that stretches to the west of Portland Street between Niagara and Queen Streets and its comfortable benches, meandering walkways, and gracious old trees have been renamed Victoria Square Park. Despite its idyllic setting, the land in Victoria Square is still officially military property owned by the Department of National Defence, but is maintained by the City of Toronto as a public park. In the early 1900s a cenotaph was erected to mark the site. The figure of a wounded soldier with his left jacket sleeve empty is a tribute to those wounded in battle and is the work of Walter Seymour Allward, a noted Canadian architect and sculptor who also designed the Vimy Memorial commemorating the Canadian troops' epic World War I victory in France.

The grounds also play a role in one of Toronto's oldest ghost stories. When the War of 1812 ended, Lieutenant Colonel Francis Battersby of the Glengarry Light Infantry Fencibles, an officer in the garrison, was posted to his native England. While he welcomed his return to family and friends, he was also confronted with a terrible dilemma. He owned two horses that had served him well during several campaigns and because he could not take them with him, he feared they would wind up in the hands of an uncaring owner. With heavy heart he led his trusted companions to the burying grounds, shot them dead, and had them buried where they fell. That story is told by an anonymous poet in a poem titled "Battersby's Horses." The last four lines read:

The Soldier in Victoria Square Memorial Park reminds us of war's grim toll and honours enlisted men wounded in battle.

> Some say that in the spring they hear
> Close by the graveyard railing
> The sound of ghostly horses' hooves
> And ghostly, plaintive neighing.

Nearby, Draper Street runs north from Front Street West to Wellington Street West between Portland Street and Spadina Avenue. It is believed to be named after William Henry Draper, a provincial politician who later served as Chief Justice of Upper Canada from 1863 to 1869. A number of semi-detached houses were erected in 1881, and more than a century later, in 1997, Heritage Toronto recommended that the entire street be designated as a Heritage Conservation District to preserve a rare surviving example of a residential street in a neighbourhood consisting mostly of industrial buildings. Draper Street runs one way north and is only 33 feet wide, half the usual road allowance width, which is part of its unique charm. It is popularly believed that the housing was built for the families of officers stationed at Fort York, but a study of the area found no evidence to substantiate this.

Draper Street is an architectural gem nestled in one of the city's oldest neighbourhoods.

Honest Ed cranks up his heater during a mound appearance at the SkyDome (now called the Rogers Centre), home to the Toronto Blue Jays.

REVIEWS, REVIVALS, DIVAS AND THE DOME

The Theatre District

The streets a few blocks east and west of Bathurst along Bloor Street are a grand jumble of clothing stores, take-out joints, restaurants, barber shops, and other contributors to the urban infrastructure, jammed with people who rush purposefully along in a New York hurry.

Over a century ago, in the 1840s, the district around Bathurst and Bloor was a thinly populated area known as the Bush, and the first substantial building to be erected was a stagecoach stop that George T. Davies built in 1876 at the intersection of Bloor and Brunswick streets. It served primarily as a hotel until the early 1950s when undergraduates at the nearby University of Toronto discovered it and the Brunswick, as it was then known, became a very popular bar. In 1961 Morris and Albert Nightingale bought the Brunswick and the venerable saloon attained a reputation that attracted youthful merrymakers from all over the city.

An area resident nicknamed "The Queen of Sweden" added to the jollity with her improvised dance routines, and patrons placed their orders with a singing waitress named Diamond Lil Sheperd who slung beer for more than 40 years. The increasing popularity of the Brunswick forced the Nightingales to put up a one-storey addition called Pickle Alley, but even that wasn't enough to accommodate the crowds. After the Colonial Tavern on Yonge Street closed in the early '70s, the Brunswick became a major centre for jazz and blues music and the nightly crowds grew even bigger. Another addition called Albert's Hall was opened, and Diamond Lil Sheperd returned from semi-retirement for the occasion to sing "Rule Britannia" and "I've Got a Lovely Bunch of Coconuts." The late wrestler Whipper Billy Watson refereed a boxing match on the main floor. *Toronto Sun* columnist Paul Rimstead conducted his highly entertaining but unsuccessful campaign for mayor from a table near the bar at the Brunswick. The late cartoonist and humanitarian Ben

Wicks used the Brunswick as headquarters during his CBC-sponsored search for the "Typical Canadian," and Irving Layton once read some of his poetry there to an admiring audience. By 1980 the Brunswick's beer sales were among the highest in the province and although competition has reduced the numbers somewhat, a staggering total is still consumed every year at the beloved institution.

Brunswick Avenue was named to honour Caroline of Brunswick–Wolfenbuttel, wife of George IV. Bloor Street gets its name from Joseph Bloor, a brewer who lived nearby. Honest Ed's Alley, one block west of Bathurst, is named after Edwin Mirvish, the guru of the garish, the businessman who wooed his customers with a hearty laugh instead of a hard sell and built a fortune doing so.

Ed was nine years old when his parents migrated from the United States to Canada in 1923. Six years later he dropped out of school to earn his living. Ed told the story of those early days, and the days that followed, in his book *Honest Ed Mirvish*, and while he frequently refers to himself as "lucky" the real reason for his success is hard work and a remarkable ability to earn free publicity. You say Honest Ed in this town and nobody has to ask, "Honest Ed who?"

In June 2004, Ed, his wife Anne, and their son David were given honourary degrees from the University of Toronto for their contributions to art and entertainment. Ed is a recipient of the Order of Canada, a Commander of the Order of the British Empire, and has been named a Freeman of the City of London, a title giving him the right to herd sheep across London Bridge without paying a toll. One is left to wonder what he could have accomplished if he *hadn't* waited until he was 15 to drop out of school.

It all began shortly after Ed married the aforementioned Anne Maklin from Hamilton. Ed rented a lockup store on the south side of Bloor just west of Bathurst. It was a tiny place, 15 feet wide and 12 feet deep, and lacking a phone, toilet, storeroom, and back door. The spaces were rented for a few months to people with goods they wanted to sell quickly. After the lease expired the owner would lock the door until the next businessman came along. Ed and Anne Mirvish stocked the shelves with women's clothing, called the place the Sport Bar, and did so well that by 1946 they owned every one of the lockup stores stretching from Bathurst west to Markham Street.

In 1948 Honest Ed's burst on the scene with all the subtlety of one of his famous Door Crasher Specials. I reported on the Door Crasher Specials many times over the years and the scenario was always the same. At the appointed hour the doors were unlocked by attendants who immediately fled for their lives while hordes of bargain seekers thundered through the aisles. It was like the running of the bulls in Spain, only more dangerous.

Honest Ed had no artistic training, but he sure knew how to draw crowds.

He staged a triplet's fashion show, sold dollar jars of coffee for 23 cents, and gave the New Year's baby its weight in silver dollars — a headline-grabbing gesture that cost him $160. On another memorable occasion he had a Noah's Ark sale including squirrel monkeys, honey bears, and a California sea lion. Larger than life photographs of Ed are plastered all over his storefront, along with various mottos like "Honest Ed Ain't Upper Crust But He Saves You Dough." He staged turkey giveaways and a "Bring Back the Prices of the '30s" event when the store sold bread for 5 cents a loaf and a bag of potatoes for 17 cents.

Ed kept expanding his operations, eventually buying up every house on the block of Markham Street adjacent to his store. All of the Victorian-era buildings were remodeled into antique stores, art galleries, and two French restaurants. The street is called Mirvish Village and its genteel ambience, coupled with the perpetual hubbub occurring next door at Honest Ed's, are a compelling combination of flair and blare that has turned the district into one of Toronto's leading tourist attractions.

In 1962 when the Royal Alexandra theatre on King Street West was up for sale, Ed made a bid for it. His offer created something of a stir as people wondered what the ringmaster of Honest Ed's would do to the gracious old building. All the other bidders made it clear they planned to tear down the building and erect something that would generate more revenue, whereas Ed wanted to restore it. The board of trustees handling the sale wanted the building retained and used as a theatre. Ed did not make his bid in person for the old theatre, afraid that if he attached his name to an offer he wouldn't stand a chance. He made his offer through an assistant, but it wasn't accepted so he launched a propaganda blitz complete with a tongue-in-cheek promise that he would not sell toothpaste in the lobby. He also promised to operate it as a live entertainment centre for at least five years even if it lost money every year.

Destruction of the building would have meant a significant loss because the "Royal Alex" is more than a theatre, it is part of Toronto's early history. It was built in 1907 on the site of the cricket field of Upper Canada College and its neighbours included Doyle's Hotel-Tavern, St. Andrew's Presbyterian Church, and the Lieutenant-Governor's mansion. Those four corners were popularly called Damnation, Salvation, Legislation, and Education. The Royal Alex cost $750,000 at the time. Stars such as Orson Welles, Paul Robeson, and Raymond Massey performed on its stage, but it gradually fell into a state of disuse and disrepair. It went on the market for $215,000 in the early 1960s.

Ed bought it in 1963 and promptly spent $750,000 restoring the lovely old building to its former glory. The renovation altered the original air conditioning system:

The Real Thing *and a highland fling are all in a day's work for Honest Ed.*

in the summer months ice had been shovelled into tanks located below the basement floor where powerful fans sucked air off the ice and blew it under the auditorium seats. The owners had claimed this clever arrangement made it the first air-conditioned building in the world. It also was said to be the first theatre in Canada to be completely fireproof.

When the curtains finally opened September 9, 1963 theatre-goers were not disappointed. The first night performance of the comedy *Never Too Late* starring William Bendix was a hit with audiences even though the play was savagely reviewed by the newspaper critics. A steady succession of first-run shows brought back patrons who had grown disenchanted with the lacklustre productions offered by the previous ownership, and a whole new generation was introduced to the delights of big-name live theatre.

Quality restaurants opened up to cater to the theatre crowd. At the height of its popularity Honest Ed's restaurant was serving thousands of roast beef dinners every Saturday night. Ed figured it would take 75 cows to provide that much beef and that got him thinking. David Mirvish said his father wanted to establish a ranch across the street and raise cattle for the restaurant. "He saw himself as the only Jewish cowboy in Toronto who herded his cattle while riding a motorcycle, but I managed to talk him out of it." David sighed and said, "I was the adult in that family."

Eventually other entertainment venues such as the Tim Sims Playhouse, Roy Thomson Hall, and the Princess of Wales Theatre (which the Mirvishes built themselves) opened their doors, and Toronto had a clearly-defined theatre district. In 1993, on the day of the press conference announcing the construction of his Princess of Wales Theatre, Ed and his son David rolled onto the scene seated 40 feet up in the bucket of a gigantic bulldozer. When the bucket touched the ground he jumped out and with a dramatic flourish pulled a lever that took the first bite out of the building site. The entrance received front-page treatment by every major news outlet in Toronto — Ed was never one to underestimate the value of free publicity.

My own theatre experience is restricted to command performances before panels of income tax investigators, but over the years I did get the opportunity to interview many of the district's biggest acts, some of whom I'd admired since childhood. When I was growing up in Hamilton my parents always took my sister, my two brothers, and me to see the latest Andy Hardy movie at the Regent Theatre on Locke Street. The title role was played by Mickey Rooney. Starlets like Ann Rutherford and Bonita Granville were romantic interests, though the love scenes amounted to little more than firm hand-shakes and expressions of goodwill. Those prim boy-girl encounters pleased my parents who were ever on the alert for corrupting influences. My folks thought those

Andy Hardy movies taught good family values, so, many a night my siblings and I sat in that movie house, dressed in our Sunday best, scrubbed clean behind the ears and listening intently.

I became a devoted admirer of Mickey Rooney, so years later when he was performing at the Royal Alex I wangled an invitation to meet him backstage. I had grown to believe that Mickey behaved just like his character so imagine my surprise when I entered his dressing room to the sight of him stroking the long blond hair of an attractive woman seated on the floor at his feet. Both were fully clad but I surmised from Mickey's soothing tone of voice that something was afoot. The mood in the room soured when my escort introduced me as a television reporter. With that, the young lady disappeared in a puff of expensive perfume and Mickey jumped to his feet demanding to know if the television camera was rolling, and if so, he wanted it turned off immediately. He was a happily married man he said, and he had no idea how the young lady had got into his room. He calmed down somewhat when I convinced him I was there only as a devoted fan, but the tone was set.

Mickey wasn't the only big name visiting Toronto in those days. Live theatre venues were showing megahits such as *Les Misérables*, *Miss Saigon*, and *Cats* and movie crews were filming all over the city. An irascible Robert Mitchum turned me down quite profanely when I asked him for an interview, but other encounters with the famous didn't go as badly. I was scheduled to interview the beloved comedian George Burns, and while that may sound glamorous, it did give rise to a troubling question. What could I possibly ask a superstar like George that hadn't been asked before? I settled for, "Mr. Burns, after all your press conferences is there a question you would like to be asked, but never have been?" "Yes," he replied, pausing for a moment before taking a cigar the size of a kayak out of his mouth, "but it wasn't that one."

I interviewed Sammy Davis Jr. on the day Elvis Presley died and we parted bitter enemies. He tried to convince me that he and Elvis used to perform together at Grossinger's Resort in the Catskills. I did not doubt the talents of the two men, but I had difficulty with the concept of a rock and roll act at Grossinger's given that the clientele is more receptive to music and humour with a Jewish flavor.

I interviewed Phyllis Diller shortly after she had undergone an extensive facelift and I don't think either one of us ever completely recovered. Her skin was bright red and as tight as a bass drum, but trouper that she is, she soldiered on, using me as a test audience for her new look. Her remarks were all quite funny, but CFTO regulations at the time expressly forbade reporters from showing emotion of any kind during an interview. Every time she knocked off a witty one-liner I would set my face in a neutral expression and press on to my next question. My lack of response irked the famous star as she was due to perform that night, but I stuck to my orders and gamely talked on without cracking a smile. This mirthless standoff continued until her assistant accidentally knocked a glass of water right into her lap to give Phyllis the out she was seeking. She jumped to her feet, let out a piercing shriek, and swept out of the room pausing only long enough to throw one of her crazy hats at me. I was going to keep the chapeau as a memento, but I got frisked on the way out and was forced to hand it over. Those big stars never throw anything away.

I interviewed Eartha Kitt on a day when something so terrible had happened to her that her vocabulary had been reduced to "yes" and "no." Things took a similar turn for the worse when I interviewed Ojibwa painter Norval Morrisseau while he was artist-in-residence at the Tom Thomson cabin on the grounds of the McMichael Canadian Art Gallery in Kleinburg. I had only been in the cabin a few minutes when he suddenly ordered me out; apparently my presence disturbed the elements. "The cameraman can stay, but you have to get out because you are too old." I conducted the interview through the cabin window.

But not all trial was without reward. Carol Channing, the Broadway star who made "Hello Dolly" and "Diamonds Are a Girl's Best Friend" her signature tunes, was in Toronto to be the glamorous spokeswoman for a jewellery retailer when I interviewed her. I know that world-weary reporters aren't supposed to admit this, but that interview was a career highlight and I still have the autographed *Hello Dolly* album she gave me.

I also had better luck when I interviewed the Australian actor Paul Hogan who was starring in the *Crocodile Dundee* movies. Though Hogan didn't enjoy being interviewed and his publicity agent had warned me that he was in a sour mood (he was responding with polite but terse answers), when I mentioned his native Australia he perked up. The country's reputation as a former penal colony meant that people once guarded their forefathers' secret pasts, but now Australians gleefully recounted their ancestors' evil deeds.

I asked Paul if he had anyone of ill repute in his own family tree. He brightened up immediately and said that unfortunately he didn't, so he had invented a relative called the Wapping Strangler. Paul discovered that as word of his fictional forefather's misdeeds got around he began getting invites to posh soirees. "The day after I mentioned to a friend that the Wapping Strangler set fire to three orphanages and the town hall, I got a letter requesting my presence at the premier social gathering in Sydney, and while that may have been a coincidence, I can tell you I have been on the cocktail circuit ever since." Paul looked right into the camera and said to me "G'day Mate," and the interview ended on that cheery note.

Uri Geller earned his international reputation as a

paranormalist who could use the power of his mind to erase computer tapes and discs, bend spoons . . . you name it. When we met in a Toronto hotel room I asked him to bend a door key my cameraman provided. He took it, softly stroked it with his long fingers, then set it on a coffee table. Nothing happened for a few minutes so he asked me to sit beside him, explaining that my presence would add to whatever mysterious powers he marshalled to perform the feat. A few moments later the key's teeth began to curl upward until they were at a right angle to the handle, and the key stayed that way. Pretty good trick.

Interviewing "ordinary" people wasn't much easier. One New Year's day I was on duty, and, as usual, the only story on the assignment sheet had to do with the New Year's baby. Other than to the immediate family, the story is of limited interest and the baby never has anything interesting to say. I decided instead to do a story on someone who had turned a great age on that day, which led me to a senior's residence on St. Clair Avenue to meet Amy Fuller. She had turned 90 and was in full command of her faculties, so, as the cameraman was setting up, I told her I was going to ask her about different aspects of life in the early 1900s. She gave thoughtful answers to all my questions, so when the cameraman signalled he was ready to roll I had reason to believe that CFTO viewers were in for an interesting glimpse into the past.

"Amy," I said, "what was your reaction the first time you saw a car?" She paused for a few seconds then said, with a touch of exasperation in her voice, that I had already asked her that question. Rallying smoothly from that setback I then inquired what a loaf of bread cost in 1915 and she proceeded to scold, "I *told* you, you've *asked* me those questions!" She commanded me to get on with things because cookies were being served shortly in the parlour and she had no intention of missing out. I didn't get a word out of Amy, but life's like that. Just when you think you have everything in apple pie order you get whacked with a lemon harangue.

My brush with the ordinary and extraordinary not only took me into the theatres and living rooms (the scene of much impromptu home theatre) of the city, it also took me to that bastion of public theatre, the sports arena. One of the grandest of these in Toronto was the SkyDome (renamed the Rogers Centre in 2005) where Canadian performers Allan Thicke, Tommy Ambrose, and Oscar Peterson celebrated the biggest attraction in Toronto the night of June 3, 1989.

Opening night meant every one of the 55,000 seats was filled for the $3.5 million dollar extravaganza. It commenced when the roof was rolled back and a team of six parachutists silently dropped from the sky. It was a damp night so they lost their footing on the rain-slick landing area while an anxious crowd looked on. Luckily, nobody was hurt and the rest of the evening

Wayne Parkes.

Song and dance preparations for the opening night gala at the SkyDome.

continued without a hitch. The roof leaked and the rain never stopped falling but everybody had a good time with the possible exception of Paul Godfrey, the chairman of the first night gala. "It's ironic the place was built to keep the bad weather out," he commented morosely, "and then they rolled back the roof and let the bad weather in."

SkyDome was hailed as the amphitheatre of the future when it opened carrying a price tag of $600 million, but new ownership acquired it in 2005 for a modest outlay of $25 million, the sort of bargain usually associated with Honest Ed. The area just a few blocks south of SkyDome, known as "the harbourfront," has suffered a similar twist of fate. American humorist Mark Twain once said everybody talks about the weather but nobody does anything about it. That is a perfect description of the tortured negotiations surrounding the eventual fate of this area.

In 1972 the federal government donated the harbour lands to the City of Toronto. While this immediately sparked talk of grandiose development, nothing happened until 1977 when Walter Oster, with the help of a bank loan, made an offer to buy the Pier 4 warehouse on Queen's Quay near Rees Street. Pier 4 was created in the early 1920s from landfill that Oster described as a mixture of mud and cinders from an old Consumer's Gas building on Front Street. Lake boats from the Grace Line tied up at the pier with their cargo, and it was a busy place until lake shipping declined. The storehouse was then used as a mail sorting facility. Oster wanted to turn it into the Pier 4 Restaurant.

When Oster's bid was accepted he became the first person to invest his own money in the harbourfront. The loan that kick-started development along the harbour area was for $5 million and his last loan, which the bank promptly approved, was for $35 million. Not bad for a man born in a modest home on Ontario Street and who dropped out of school after Grade 10.

Peir 4.

Harbourfront Pier 4 under construction.

By the early 1970s businesses along Spadina Avenue heralded a global village.

RAG TRADE AND REBELLION

Spadina and Kensington

Shortly before the onset of the War of 1812 Doctor W.W. Baldwin built a house he named Spadina, the Indian word for hill (pronounced Spadeena), on a rise of land just east of where Casa Loma now stands. The house is gone, but it was an imposing residence with two parlours on one floor, four bedrooms and a study on another, and several rooms in the basement including a kitchen, dairy, and a wine cellar. From the house he had a clear view to Lake Ontario. A few years after moving in he laid out a broad avenue 131 feet across, which was later expanded to its existing width of 160 feet. The generous width of the sidewalks provide plenty of room for walking, shopping, selling, or for people with stories to tell.

Jack Kent Cooke is remembered now as the U.S.-based owner of the Washington Redskins football team, but back in the 1950s and 1960s he was a flamboyant Toronto businessman who owned high profile properties such as radio station CKEY and the Toronto Maple Leafs (of the old International Baseball League). Cooke went on to make his fortune in the United States, but on a trip back to Toronto he told reporters he visited the Victory Burlesque on Spadina at Dundas, seeking "creative inspiration" while observing the ostrich feathers and garter belts that fleetingly adorned the talented performers who graced the stage. Cooke was already a millionaire, so I did a story based on the theory that if watching exotic dancers was the key to great wealth I would visit the Victory and start my voyage to the good life.

Monica Kennedy was the star attraction that week. She believed her starring role at the Victory would get her back on the road to stardom and if a television appearance would speed matters along she was only too happy to oblige. I did not interview Monica in her working costume; instead she donned a white robe that covered her from head to toe. Despite this safeguard, when the item went to air that night the newsroom was

The Victory Burlesque offered its own version of local colour.

flooded with calls from irate viewers. From then on I tried to keep the concerns of parents and more conservative audience members in mind.

Spadina is also home to Joe Heller and Federal Printing. In 1937 Joe took over the business that his father David established in 1931, a step up from his old occupation of selling fresh fish door to door. The printing game wasn't his son's first choice either. Joe's first job was in a soap works and one of his duties was to take the weekly cash deposit to a nearby bank. It was a simple task with a set routine that took him through a pretty tough neighbourhood, and Joe did it without incident for several weeks. But fearful that the odds were against him, Joe returned from his bank trip one day and handed in the briefcase, the deposit slip, and his resignation and joined the family firm. His business neighbours included Kazden Groceries, Friedland's Textiles, Grossman's Tavern (the first bar in Toronto to serve draft beer in jugs), and Kwinter's Eggs, whose workforce of women did nothing but break eggs all day, and while it wasn't a noisy business, it certainly created a pungent smell.

Grossman's is at the corner of Spadina and Cecil, and it too has a smell and a sound all its own. Jazz, folk, and rock musicians have performed for more than 30 years in an atmosphere redolent with roasted peanuts, beer, and tobacco. The tables are small, although there's more room on them, now that ashtrays aren't needed, the chairs are rickety and uncomfortable, but the patrons are hardy souls and nobody seems to mind. Kid Bastien and his New Orleans jazz band The Happy Pals were fixtures at Grossman's for almost a quarter of a century, and when Kid died on February 8, 2003, I was among the mourners who celebrated his life at a traditional jazzman's send-off.

A few doors south of Federal Printing is another business dating back to Spadina's early days. Israel Rotman purchased the building at 345 Spadina in 1944 for $2800 and opened Rotman's Hats. His son David

John Rygh.

Grossman's Tavern, the home of the blues, has been a Spadina Avenue fixture for more than half a century.

has been running the store since 1964. Not that there's that much to run anymore, David says, because John Kennedy killed the hat business when he showed up bare-headed for his presidential inauguration in 1962. David is still pretty miffed at the late president, but he shows up to work every day ready to avail customers of his considerable knowledge of Trilbys and top hats. And, ever the optimistic salesman, David believes hats are on the verge of a comeback because people are buying them for shade and UV protection.

Rotman's was not the only hat store on Spadina Avenue. One of his business rivals was the late Sammy Taft, an ebullient man with a well-developed sense of self-promotion. Sammy used to sit on an old wooden stool outside his store talking to everybody who passed by, and sooner or later the conversation always got around to hats, Sammy's hats. He opened his business in 1932, and visiting sports stars and show biz personalities invariably found the time to drop in to his store and swap stories.

The walls of the store were lined with photographs, a veritable who's who: boxing champ Joe Louis, a young Gordie Howe, Jack Benny, Bob Hope, Guy Lombardo, and dozens of others. Sammy didn't advertise very much because he believed in "word of head." Every visiting celebrity was given a hat as he left the premises and it paid off, because at the height of his business he sold thousands of fedoras, berets, and bowlers every year. In

Diagonal parking added to the Spadina traffic chaos in front of Rotman's, but few seemed to mind.

Toronto, men's hats were popularly called "Sammies."

Sammy had many comedians in his wide circle of friends and he liked to write jokes for them when they came to Toronto to perform. One year Phil Silvers headlined the annual Canadian National Exhibition and Sammy supplied him with several one-liners. I interviewed the colourful hat salesman not long afterward and asked him for an example of the material. His reply was included in my report when it aired on that evening's newscast: "Phil told the audience he had a bet on a horse at 20 to one and it didn't come in until quarter to three." Sammy then said with perfect timing and a straight face that Phil bombed despite his contributions.

Switzer's Deli and Shopsy's were two other dependable sources for my "kickers." Switzer's was located on the west side of Spadina and Shopsy's was directly across the street. They both served tasty corned beef on rye sandwiches, matzo ball soup, dill pickles, and other wonderful Jewish fare. Switzer's small, crowded, and dark interior — not to mention the efficient staff who shouted orders to the chef who whipped them up with astonishing speed — was the quintessential deli experience. Requests for a little extra mustard for the pastrami or some applesauce with your blintzes were unfailingly fulfilled. It was the kind of place you just felt good going into.

The same held for Shopsy's, though for different reasons. Sam Shopsowitz and his brother Israel were

Shopsy's.

*Sam (Shopsy) Shopsowitz serves up the house
specialty to Johnny Wayne and Frank Shuster.*

Shopsy's.

*I deliver flowers to actor Al Waxman during a daffodil
campaign to raise funds for cancer research.*

both active in the Variety Club, so famous performers were frequent customers in their bright, modern premises. Comedian Danny Kaye was a regular, and the place always overflowed with fans and friends when he swept into the room.

One day when I was in there I asked the Canadian impressionist Rich Little to imitate my voice and do the sign-off at the end of my report. It took him two tries, but then the words "Glenn Cochrane, CFTO News," came out of his mouth and it sounded better than when I said it. In private conversation Rich was a delightful raconteur who loved telling Hollywood stories. They were always amusing, and if he was telling a story involving Humphrey Bogart and Cary Grant he would use their voices — it was like actually being there. Switzer's has moved to the northern reaches of Toronto, and Shopsy's relocated to Front Street across from the Hockey Hall of Fame, but that doesn't mean things have quieted down on the old thoroughfare.

A small neon sign reading OPEN SUNDAY is displayed in the window of a Victorian-era house at 202 Spadina Avenue. The ground floor of the building has been occupied since 1959 by Paul Magder Furs and that small sign, which is only worth about $200, eventually cost him $200,000 in legal fees, and countless hours spent fighting authorities over his right to stay open for business on Sundays. The genesis of that battle originated in 1906 when the federal government passed the Lord's

John Rygh.

Paul Magder was open for business to Sunday shoppers despite frequent police visits to his Spadina Avenue storefront.

Day Alliance Act banning commercial activity on Sunday. For years it was the ironclad law of the land, but gradually individual provinces were granted exemptions. Sunday sports came to Ontario in 1950, movie theatres followed in 1961, and in 1967 restaurants could serve alcohol on a Sunday, though you had to order a meal to go with it. By 1968 it became legal to go to a horse track on a Sunday as long as the first race didn't begin until 1:30 p.m.

However, the matter of Sunday shopping remained a potentially explosive issue. The city tiptoed into those chilly waters by declaring certain parts of the city to be tourist areas and therefore exempt from Sunday closing laws. One of those areas was Chinatown West, which stretched from Queen Street north to College Street. Paul Magder Furs is located a few blocks north of Queen, and since that falls within the boundaries of Chinatown West, Madger felt his business also merited the exemption. The authorities disagreed, but by mid-1971 Magder had had enough of what he considered to be a discriminatory practice and he decided to challenge the law.

He proceeded with such relentless vigour that in four years he had accumulated more than 200 charges under the Retail Business Holidays Act and faced fines of more than $2 million (only $9,000 of which he actually paid). The battle was watched closely because of its potential influence on Sunday shopping patterns, and coverage of Magder's weekly skirmishes with authorities were a staple in the media.

Magder is a tall, strongly built man, and many a Sunday I reported on his scuffles with the police as he tried to keep the store open. He lost his temper more than once, but he never lost his sense of humour, at one point telling a judge that the fines he was getting forced him to stay open on Sunday so he could pay them! Eventually the uproar subsided and old enemies were forgiven, including the police. In fact, they brought him a cake on the tenth anniversary of the first ticket he was given. The matter has never been officially resolved;

he just stopped getting charged. He remains obsessed with those long ago battles, but he also has a sense of satisfaction. "I wasn't the one who brought about Sunday shopping," he told me once, "but I did speed up the process."

Magder's wasn't the only battle being fought on Spadina in those days. There was monumental uproar over a proposal to bring the Spadina Expressway down from the north, which would cut a swath along the street that would obliterate its busy life. Bowing to citizen concern, on June 3, 1971, Ontario Premier Bill Davis announced that the Spadina Expressway would end at Lawrence Avenue. He made the announcement with a rhetorical flair that is seldom heard in the Ontario legislature. "If we are building a transportation system to serve the automobile, then the Spadina Expressway would be a good place to start. But if we are building a transportation system to serve people, then Spadina is a good place to stop."

Spadina is synonymous with sweat and hard labour, but there is also an elegant side to the old thoroughfare that has largely been forgotten. Spadina had its beginnings when the Jewish tradesmen who initially made up most of the workforce in the garment industry eventually moved from making clothes to designing them. Thriving factories such as the Fashion Building and the Balfour Building were erected on Spadina Avenue during the 1920s. The Balfour Building was named in honour of the former British prime minister who in 1917 committed his government to support a Jewish homeland in Palestine. Other notable structures include the Darling Building, one of the first fireproof factories in Toronto and home of the Darling Dress Company, and the Tower Building, occupied mainly by small companies producing ladies' cloaks, suits, and dresses.

Those imposing old workplaces are a reminder of the times when Spadina turned out quality garments created by Canadian designers like Gertrude Kahan and Marilyn Brooks. Every year the industry sponsored gala award nights and coveted gilt statuettes were handed out to winners in a number of categories. The statuettes were called Judy, the clothing industry's nickname for a dressmaker's dummy. Marilyn Brooks was a former Judy winner and remembers the 1960s fondly, especially as the industry feted its leaders with glamorous celebrations at the Royal York Hotel. Spadina lost its cachet as the hub of the garment trade when manufacturers began moving their operations to the suburbs where land was cheaper. Those heady days are remembered by a simple monument that stands on the northwest corner of Spadina Avenue and Richmond Street — titled Uniform Measuring Stack, it consists of a stone thimble sitting atop a pile of six dressmaker's buttons, also made of stone. Two other buttons lie scattered on the sidewalk a few feet from the pile. They are mute reminders of the

Winners at the garment gala receive a "Judy," the industry nickname for a tailor's dummy.

Marilyn Brooks.

The Uniform Measuring Stack is a monument to generations of workers who toiled in the garment district.

hectic working conditions in those long-ago factories.

Kensington Market is located in an area one block west of Spadina. The market was created in part by the Toronto fire of 1904 that destroyed the downtown business district. When it came time to rebuild, many companies relocated their factories along the south end of Spadina Avenue, where land was cheaper. At that time Jewish refugees fleeing the pogroms in Eastern Europe began arriving in Toronto. They found jobs in the sewing trade on Spadina Avenue and a few blocks away, on streets such as Kensington, Baldwin, and Augusta, they found affordable housing. Material possessions were limited to bare essentials, jobs were low-paying with no chance for advancement, and prejudice was a daily reality. It was an existence made more livable by the currency of favours, a pattern that continued as new immigrants arrived from new places.

Neighbours pitched in when somebody wanted to turn the ground floor of a house into a small store. Several synagogues were established, kosher stores and kosher butchers set up businesses, and Kensington and its market were born. When the Grossberger family started a grocery store on Augusta Street, despite knowing not a word of English, nearby residents came in with containers of various products to show them what it was they wanted to buy.

The Jewish population in the area has declined gradually so that today only two synagogues remain. The

Produce is still plentiful and fresh in Kensington Market, although prices have gone up since this 1973 photo.

Kiever, located at Bellevue Avenue and Denison Square, is the first Jewish structure in Toronto to be given an historical building designation. A statue of the late actor Al Waxman stands in the square across the street from the synagogue. He never lived in Kensington, but he starred in the long-running television series *King of Kensington*, which brought added recognition to the area.

When the Sanci family wanted to establish a banana store that grew into a tropical food outlet, businesses in the ultra-competitive area readily made room for them. Melons were sold in many locations in the market and every proprietor claimed to have an infallible way of telling when a melon was ripe. Some tapped it lightly with a forefinger, some rotated it for one or two minutes, others shook it to determine if it gurgled, and everyone maintained their method was infallible. I tried them all and I still can't tell when a melon is ready to eat. I haven't had any luck detecting the perfect fig either, despite the efforts of cameraman George Stamou, a Greek who learned the food lore of colour and texture in the family business and conducted noisy arguments with Kensington vendors.

Tiger Armstrong ran a wildly popular café-cum-drop-in centre on Kensington Avenue called Tiger's Coconut Grove. Tiger made "the best pina colada that ever slid down a throat," and was a charming host who always found time for his customers. Tiger also was the softest touch in Kensington market, and Toronto is full of former students and struggling actors and musicians who will tell you that Tiger supported them through many a bad patch. Tiger, with his big, broad smile and lilting Jamaican accent, is long gone from Kensington along with many of the Jewish merchants who originally gave the area its distinctive flavour.

Other European and African immigrant populations replaced them and the market evolved. Mario Tomaz, who ran the Portuguese bookstore for many years, is a perfect example. Every Sunday he would hook up a loudspeaker to his short-wave radio so homesick Portuguese immigrants could listen to the weekly soccer match.

I used to lead historic walks through the market. When the tour was finished I would always quote that old phrase, "It takes a village to raise a child," adding that it takes a lot of children to raise a village. Sam Lunansky said whenever he entered the streets of Kensington he always felt safe. Those first immigrants created a haven for themselves, but they also created a unique and much-loved part of Toronto that lives in the hearts of many.

Generations of Canadian soldiers trained at the Armouries on University Avenue.

Mike Filey

THE GREAT DIVIDE

Yonge Street

For many years the public perception of University Avenue was shaped by the glowering bulk of the University Avenue Armouries. The building was demolished in 1963, and today the north-south artery is better known as the route of the annual Santa Claus parade.

The 100th anniversary of the beloved extravaganza, complete with scores of floats and hundreds of participants, was held November 21, 2004. The first parade started on Front Street and took a circuitous route through the downtown area before winding up at Eaton's on Queen Street where Santa was greeted by Timothy Eaton, the founder of the merchandising empire. The parade had to take a roundabout course to avoid the section of downtown still being rebuilt after the Great Toronto fire of 1904. In 1919, Santa arrived in a plane piloted by one of the greatest heroes in the country's military history, World War I flying ace and Victoria Cross recipient Billy Bishop. By 1925 the parade was so popular that the floats were shipped to Montreal the week after the Toronto event and the whole attraction was held all over again. This practice continued until the 1960s when it was halted due to the threat posed by the FLQ bombings in Quebec.

The number of floats and participants, the length of the parade, and the time it takes to traverse its route have all been duly chronicled, but one fact not generally known is that the parade is actually held twice every year in Toronto. Hundreds of thousands show up to watch as it wends its magical way from Bloor Street near Christie down University past the Hospital for Sick Children, but there is another, ghostly version held the night before, when the floats glide soundlessly down to the official starting point from the Sheppard Avenue warehouse where they are built and stored.

This was one of Jim Carmichael's favourite memories from his years as parade director. "The police lead the way downtown in the middle of the night stopping traffic and making sure the road was clear for us. A lot of people who lived along the route got used to our late-night show and would stay up until one or two in the morning to watch the floats without a single person on them." Jim is retired and the Eaton's Santa Claus Parade is now run by a consortium of advertisers who sponsor this beloved tradition. Almost as soon as the Santa Claus parade is over, construction for the next year's floats begins.

One July, I decided to do a story on preparations for the following winter, promising I wouldn't reveal too many secrets. I did the "stand up" report at the end of my story in front of the Big Bad Wolf float, a wonderful piece of mechanical ingenuity featuring a huge wolf that eventually blew down the house belonging to the Three Little Pigs. I made my remarks while all the ruckus went on behind me, and when the walls came tumbling down I was amazed to see a young woman standing unscathed amid the wreckage. As the dust settled, I looked at her and said with mock astonishment, "I don't know where they came from." This was a tagline I became associated with for many years.

Our son Ralph was dressed in a riding costume complete with a black helmet and riding jacket his first year in the parade. There is no warmer feeling for a parent than to be standing on University Avenue on a cold winter day watching your child march by in the Eaton's Santa Claus parade. Ralph, however, didn't *seem*

*My son Ralph steps in to launch my coverage of the 1975
Santa Claus parade.*

particularly impressed by it or by the $5 he received for his participation at the end of proceedings. When we got home, however, he jumped out of the car, waved the money over his head, and shouted, "I'm rich, I'm rich! I got five dollars for being in the Santa Claus parade!" It was a bravura performance that woke up the whole neighbourhood, but he never repeated it; from then on Eaton's only gave out merchandise vouchers.

Over the years I reported on many events that took place in the downtown area, but the colourful Canadian Cancer Society Daffodil Day Parade was my favourite. The parades were organized by Mary McInnis, sister to Barbara Hamilton, the much-loved Toronto theatrical performer who appeared in venues across the country. As on the day of the first parade in 1954, it started at exactly one minute before noon from Bloor Street and Devonshire Place then made its way south on Bay Street before dispersing at Simcoe Street.

In 1974 I was invited to ride down Bay Street in a convertible with Bobby Ashe, star of CFTO's *Uncle Bobby's Children's Show*. We were carrying placards with our names on them and somehow I managed to whack Bobby right on the nose with mine causing him to bleed profusely the length of the parade route. Fans called his name as we proceeded and he acknowledged every salutation, taking his bloodstained hankie away from his nose just long enough to wave a cheery hello before clamping the makeshift bandage back in place.

Yonge Street just begs for a parade, given that it is listed in *The Guinness Book of World Records* as the longest street in the world because it stretches 1,178.3 miles from Queen's Quay to Rainy River, Ontario. For all that, it hasn't really transported Torontonians to a

Metro International Caravan founders Zena and Leon Kossar are presented to Queen Elizabeth. Toronto Mayor Art Eggleton is at Her Majesty's side.

place that has captured their imaginations. The down-town intersections at King and Queen have never developed a personality that could be termed welcoming, and the porn shops and strip clubs a little farther north simply prove that there is more blight than light on what should be an exciting multi-faceted part of the city's downtown core.

Yonge Street did have an unofficial role for many years when it served as a psychological divide separating east and west Toronto. Eastenders mostly kept to them-selves and so did their fellow citizens in the west, but all that changed in 1968 when the late Leon Kossar and his wife Zena launched Caravan. Leon had moved from Winnipeg to Toronto where he wrote a column in the *Toronto Telegram*, reporting on various ethnic functions in the city. Zena was the chief accountant for the Toronto Symphony Orchestra and used to accompany Leon when researching his reports. Zena grew up in the tiny town of Arran, Saskatchewan, proud home to five grain elevators. "I recognized that same sort of pride of place when I met the people Leon was writing stories about."

The Kossars felt the time was ripe to promote that pride and move culture out of church basements and onto a larger stage. They believed that the colourful music and dance, and unfamiliar but tasty food would appeal to general audiences and build respect for other cultures in the aftermath of World War II. Their first ventures included "Easter Round the World," held in the International Institute building on College Street; "Christmas Round the World;" and a Labour Day performance at the Ex in 1967 called "The Nation Builders Show." They were well received, so the stage was set for the launch of International Caravan in 1968.

Like many good ideas, Caravan had a simple structure. Tourists bought passports that got them into 30 pavilions scattered around the city. Once inside, they could enjoy free entertainment and purchase food, drink, and inexpensive souvenirs, many of them handmade by the hardworking volunteers who were the backbone of the entire operation.

By 1980 there were 57 pavilions and Caravan's international flavour included the Polish pavilion at Dovercourt and Queen, the African one on George Street, the Italian one on Grace Street, and the Ukrainian pavilion on Manning Avenue. The nine-day event also spanned east of Yonge Street where revellers could get a taste of Macedonian, Japanese, Belgian, and Scottish cultures — all on the same night with one five-dollar passport. Caravan-goers could travel from India to the Philippines in less than half an hour. Premier Bill Davis recommended the mango juice at the New Delhi pavilion and spoke well of the entertainment — but did not comment on the Ankara pavilion, which featured a belly dancer in black veils.

Newfoundland was the first province to be represented with a pavilion on Yonge Street. The organizers

Scottish dancers fling caution to the wind and step up to perform at Caravan.

shipped fishing nets, lobster traps, 6000 pounds of cod, and 5000 bottles of beer in preparation for the evening shows featuring tap dancers, accordion players, and a charismatic soloist billed as the virtuoso of the musical spoons.

Toronto's notoriously rigid drinking laws changed in 1965 when taverns were allowed to open from noon to midnight, but they had to close from 6:30 p.m. to 8:00 p.m. In 1972 Ladies and Escorts entrances were abolished as a result of anti-discrimination laws, and in that same period restaurants were finally given permission to stage fashion shows on their premises. LCBO customers had to fill out order forms indicating the stock number, the quantity desired, the type of liquor, and the price. The clerk then processed the order and, after a lengthy search among the shelves, the clerk handed over the liquor in a discreet brown paper bag. The customer was permitted to take his purchase home where he no doubt poured himself a stiff drink after all that hassle.

The Berlin pavilion at its Club Harmonie headquarters on Sherbourne Street was a huge favourite and one night when the crowd spilled out onto the front lawn, management set up tables and began serving bratwurst and beer outdoors. People behaved themselves, the world didn't come to an end despite the predictions of the blue-stocking brigade, and now patios are a standard fixture of licensed establishments all over Toronto.

Ontario Premier Bill Davis shares the spotlight with Zena Kossar during the festival.

Caravan's volunteers were another reason for its success. I refer not only to the young men and women who spent hours perfecting the songs and dances that delighted audiences, but to the unsung efforts of women like the "perogie ladies" who began making food several weeks prior to the event and storing it in home freezers until the pavilions opened. Tonia Mykolyshyn, now a clear-minded and energetic 93 year old, volunteered for years at the Odessa Pavilion on Spadina Avenue as part of a team of 60 preparing 30,000 perogies. Tons of potatoes were peeled and mashed by hand (until someone donated a mashing machine), cabbage leaves were separated and steamed for mountains of cabbage rolls. "We stored them everywhere," Tonia remembers. "Some we took home, some we left with neighbours, and others were stored in churches and grocery stores. It was a group effort then, but life is different now. People are too busy doing other things and everybody wants to get paid for their work."

One night my cameraman and I went to a pavilion in an Italian church in Little Italy noted for the quality of the entertainment and for its spaghetti and meatballs. I arrived at the pavilion and was escorted to the kitchen where a dozen women were stirring large vats brimming with the house specialty. Just as the cameraman was setting up to shoot film, one of the women spotted me and cried out, "You were my father's favourite television announcer. He died a week ago tonight." With that, the unhappy woman burst into tears and before I knew it the entire room was filled with sobbing Italians. Unable to stem the flow of grief, I fled the premises.

The dream that Leon and Zena Kossar realized when they created Caravan built bridges between people, adding more to the soul of the city than any skyscraper could. That said, interest in Caravan waned over the years as stores and restaurants offering cuisine and goods from every culture proliferated. Caravan was dealt its final blow by the SARS outbreak in 2003.

But the festive atmosphere on Yonge was not limited to Caravan alone. In the early 1970s a portion of Yonge Street from Gerrard south to King Street was made vehicle-free during the summer months and the Yonge Street Mall was established. The idea was an instant hit with tourists and residents alike. Several entrepreneurs set up businesses catering to the throngs, but the crowds were not viewed kindly by the police, who found it difficult to maintain law and order. Authorities turned a blind eye to most of the goings on, but they drew the line when it came to the owner of a makeshift movie house showing *Deep Throat*. The scandalous porn film was banned in Ontario so the cops seized the film. Every time this happened the operator ran a fresh copy, which would in turn be confiscated. Tiring of this game, the police started seizing the movie projectors, and eventually the struggle took on a life of its own far

The crowds begin to gather in front of Eaton's on James Street for the 1972 Yonge Street Mall.

more exciting than the steamy movie itself.

Every morning a spokesman would emerge from the theatre and announce the show would be starting in ten minutes, at which point several uniformed officers would rush past him and seize the projector. After a brief delay the spokesman would re-appear and announce the start of another viewing. Again a phalanx of bluecoats would charge into the theatre and put the collar on the movie machine. Large crowds gathered daily to watch this improvised street theatre.

One day I visited the scene with a cameraman. We had only been there a few minutes when a backpacker approached me and asked if I would like him to streak past the camera. I said yes, and thought nothing more of it. In those days people were always suggesting weird stunts to me and the fad of men shedding their clothes and streaking about in public was more common than you'd think. A few minutes later the young fellow dashed past the camera stark naked except for a pair of well-worn hiking boots. A great cacophony of shouts and cheers erupted and salespeople ran out of nearby stores to see what the fuss was all about.

If the clerks were out on the street, there was nobody minding the store, so thieves sidled into the empty shops and began stealing everything in sight. The clerks realized their error and hurried back to the stores only to collide with thieves laden with all manner of pilfered merchandise. What with collisions and projector seizures and the streaker, a great confusion arose, during the course of which four people were slightly injured and several arrests were made. The police managed to get the mall closed not long after, citing an increase in crime. I apologize to the citizens of Toronto if I had inadvertently contributed when I gave the streaker the green light.

Yonge had a sleazy collection of massage parlours, strip bars, and porno stores, but for many years it also provided a haven for young women new to Toronto looking for work. The Women's Christian Temperance Union building just around the corner at 20 Gerrard Street offered room and board for $50 a month, no male visitors, no booze in the building, and residents who were out after 11:00 p.m. had to sign in at the front desk. The WCTU formed in the late 1890s to support the temperance movement and to campaign to give women the right to vote. The two goals were united in their belief that women would vote against demon drink. When Gwen Egan came from Unity, Saskatchewan in the early 1950s to study at the Ontario College of Art, she called the place the Wack-a-too, and other residents claimed the initials on the sign outside stood for Whisky Can't Touch Us. As for whisky and other potables, Ms. Egan says it was easy to smuggle in because the ladies on the front desk couldn't recognize a liquor store bag if you pulled one over their heads.

Ms. Egan remembers Yonge Street in that era as an inexpensive, interesting, and relatively safe place for young women as long as they ignored the wolf whistles directed their way. A bowl of soup with toast cost 50 cents at Basel's restaurant on Yonge Street near Gerrard, and the Zanzibar Tavern was a pleasant place for a drink. According to the law of the day, if you wanted to drink you had to eat, so the Zanzibar had a circulating ham sandwich that accompanied every booze order. Nobody ever actually ate it; the sandwich just stayed on the table until it was needed elsewhere.

City of Toronto Archives.

The Bloor Street viaduct linked east and west and vitalized neighbourhoods on both sides of the valley.

BALDY AND THE BRIDGE

Cabbagetown and the Danforth

Today the Don Valley hosts the parkway that runs along its floor starting from the Gardiner Expressway and heads north to Newmarket and beyond, carrying thousands of vehicles into and out of the downtown area, but early in Toronto's history its natural beauty served very different purposes. Governor John Graves Simcoe and his family enjoyed frequent picnics on a hill overlooking the Don River, and Simcoe's wife, Elizabeth, eventually built a cabin on the site named Castle Frank after their son Francis.

Francis joined the army after the family returned to England in 1796 and was killed in action during the Spanish Peninsular War. The Valley had a natural beauty, but it was not a popular destination — with good reason. In the 1850s a group of desperadoes called the Brooks Bush Gang lurked in the woods and robbed unsuspecting passersby. Whenever they obtained enough money from these nefarious activities they gambled it at Jack Maitland's racetrack at Broad-view and Eastern Avenues. If they had any money left, it was spent at the Butcher's Arms on Mill's Lane, now Broadview Avenue, which was famous for its weekly cockfights.

In 1915 work began on a bridge spanning the valley from Broadview to Parliament. When completed, it stretched 1,620 feet across the valley, with a subway line running underneath the car traffic. Originally called the Bloor-Danforth Viaduct, the name was changed to the Prince Edward Viaduct after that member of the royal family took a car trip across the span when it was opened in 1919. If the Prince had continued his ride and turned left on Parliament Street at the Castle Frank subway station he would have arrived in an old and picturesque district called Cabbagetown.

Cabbagetown is also the title of a book, written by the late novelist Hugh Garner, chronicling life on its shabby streets during the Depression. This image shaped Canadians' and tourists' impression of the place, a fact that still bothers long-time Cabbagetown residents who remember their neighbourhood with genuine fondness.

The Cabbagetown Business Improvement Association defines the area between Parliament Street, the Don River, Gerrard Street, and Wellesley as the official Cabbagetown, though agreement on these boundaries is not unanimous. The area was settled by people fleeing the Irish potato famine, and by the late 1800s the population was mostly Protestant with a sizeable Roman Catholic minority. Those early arrivals dug up their front yards and planted cabbages, which gave the area its name — although some residents say it was the smell of the area, which resembled cooking cabbage, that led to the nickname. Yet another school of thought maintains that the name comes from skunk cabbages that grew in nearby fields. It is wisest just to accept whichever version one is told at the time.

Cabbagetown was a tough place and it bred tough guys, residents like local hero Albert "Frenchy" Belanger who became flyweight champion of the world in 1927 when he defeated Ernie Jarvis of England. Over the next three years Frenchy made more than $90,000 with his ring skills, a huge sum in those days, but by 1934 he was working as a waiter in a Cabbagetown beer parlour. Frenchy met Howard "Baldy" Chard, a big, quick-tempered, and fearless unofficial heavyweight champion who made a steady living as a "freelance" fist fighter in the 1950s and 1960s. When young bloods, drunk on payday, got into fights, they broke noses, jaws, beer glasses, and furniture, which didn't sit too well with management. Baldy was hired to clean out the trouble-makers, but he also ran a "boozecan" at Parliament and Dundas Streets that attracted rounders from all over the city. Baldy was also popular with the local police because they knew where to go when they were looking for "a person of interest." The old brawler eventually lost work when bar owners encouraged feuding men and women to deal diplomatically with their problems rather than be tossed out.

Baldy represented just one side of Cabbagetown according to long-time resident Linda Dixon. "Being tough was a survival technique, but at heart Cabbage-town was a close community where children played in the streets and many people never locked their doors." She recalls going to the Toy Dances, a Cabbagetown institution organized by the late Tommy Crewe in the 1960s. The admission was one toy, and by the end of the evening dolls, stuffed bears, toy soldiers, and other playthings were bundled up and delivered to needy kids at Christmas.

The Riverdale Zoo also drew children to its farm grounds until it closed in 1974 and the animals were moved to the Toronto Zoo in Scarborough. Riverdale Farm opened in 1978 and still attracts crowds of all ages.

Community activist Joice Guspie says that closeness still exists, but the ambience changed in the early 1970s when house hunters discovered the wonderful trove of

John Rygh.

Winchester Street in Cabbagetown is lined with elegantly restored Victorian-era homes.

John Rygh.

The majestic Clydesdale draught horses are a popular attraction at the Riverdale Zoo.

Victorian homes dating back to the 1870s. Renovators restored them to their former glory and a boom started that transformed many of the old neighbourhoods. Upscale retailers began setting up shop along Parliament Street and many of the new residents more used to shopping in malls sent family-owned retailers elsewhere. The Kresge's store on Parliament closed for lack of customers and several small businesses soon followed suit, paving the way for chain store operators.

One business that has remained is the St. Jamestown Steak and Chop meat store at 516 Parliament, which was run from 1971 to 2004 by a man known to generations of Cabbagetowners as Terry the Butcher. The store is the unofficial drop-in centre for the neighbourhood. During a power failure in 2002, every customer who came in the store had their order filled with the understanding that the amount owing would be paid when the lights came back on. That's what happened said Terry's son, Mark Michelin: "We weren't really taking a chance because we knew everybody."

On December 4, 1984, during one of the warmest winters in Toronto's history with temperatures hovering around the 65-degree mark, I borrowed an antique bathtub from Pat O'Dell, owner of the Cabbagetown Bath Shoppe, filled it with water and plopped in, accompanied by one of O'Dell's female friends. A photograph of the publicity stunt appeared the next day on the front page of the *Toronto Sun*.

John Rygh.

St. Jamestown Steak & Chops on Parliament Street has been a local meeting place for generations of neighbourhood shoppers.

Mike Peake, Sun.

Rub a dub dub, I climbed into a tub one balmy day in December, 1982.

Meanwhile on the other side of the valley and the bridge, several streets north and several decades earlier, that other neighbourhood linked by the viaduct was starting to take shape. By 1913 Danforth Avenue had been paved only as far as Pape Avenue, beyond that was a rutted trail running through scrubland all the way to Kingston Road. The W. Harris and Company glue factory operated for years at the corner of Danforth and Coxwell Avenue and the smell was so bad that Don Jail prisoners had their terms reduced if they agreed to work at the plant. There were few takers.

The Playter Estates just north of the Danforth and east of Broadview ridge give a much better impression of the area. A walk around its winding streets provides a look at some of its earliest history. George Playter and his family were United Empire Loyalists who left Pennsylvania in 1796 after the American Revolutionary War and were given land grants in the Don Valley area. One of his descendants built Playter House in 1871 and the handsome residence still stands at 28 Playter Crescent.

There has been a Greek presence in the area for many years, but the big influx came in the early 1950s when many Greeks left their homeland in the aftermath of the Greek Civil War of 1945–49. They moved into houses north and south of Danforth Avenue and gradually the blocks between Pape and Broadview Avenues began to fill with fish stores, bakeries, clothing stores,

The Player family, seen gathered on the front lawn of one of their earlier homesteads, set the social standard in the neighbourhood at the time.

Beach Mirror.

Greeks of all ages celebrate the face of a nation in the old world and new.

fruit stores, and restaurants serving Hellenic delights such as souvlaki, Greek salad, and baklava. Ellas, on Pape Avenue, a few doors north of the Danforth, offered avgolemono soup, fricasseed lamb, big Greek olives, and the ever-attentive presence of two waiters named Louie and Bobbi. Whenever my wife and I came for dinner (we dined there so often that one of the dishes on the menu was "Glenn Cochrane's dolmades"), Louie greeted us as if it had been years since last we met. Once seated, glasses of ouzo appeared unbidden at our table and Bobbi made sure that they were never empty. When Ellas closed in 2003 we mourned it as one does the loss of an old friend.

Beach Mirror.

Beach Mirror.

Everybody wants a Taste of the Danforth.

Toronto's interest in all things Greek led to the 1994 launch of that explosion of unfettered exuberance called the Taste of the Danforth. A bust of Alexander the Great overlooks the intersection of Danforth and Logan, and in the festival's first year, Alexander looked out at a slim crowd of 5,000 fair-goers who milled about not knowing what to expect. Ten years later Alexander's ragtag band had swelled to a throng of over one million, and for one glorious weekend in August the air is redolent with the seductive smells of Greek cooking and the skies resound with cries of "Opa!" The Taste of the Danforth festival does more than raise spirits throughout the city, it also raises money for a number of organizations, and the chief benefactor has been the Toronto East General Hospital, which has received a significant portion of the $600,000 raised to date.

The annual parade in May to mark the independence of Greece from the Ottoman Empire in 1821 has become another major event in Greektown that draws thousands of Canadians of Greek ancestry to the bustling neighbourhood.

Children flag down onlookers at the Greek Independence Day parade.

Every season brings its own beauty to the boardwalk.

John Dowding.

RED ROCKETS AND ALL THAT JAZZ

The Beach

My wife and I moved to the east end in 1970. My elderly neighbour at the time often said she was "going to the city" during our back-fence chats; she was referring to downtown Toronto. That sense of separation still exists today, in part due to the residents' stubborn defense of their territory from the excesses of development that have been inflicted on less vigilant neighbourhoods.

The Ashbridge family, Empire Loyalists who arrived in York County from Pennsylvania in 1793, were among the first in the area. Three years later the family was granted 600 acres extending from Ashbridge's Bay to Queen Street East. Their first house was built from trees cut on the property. Then in 1809 Jonathon Ashbridge started construction of a frame house for his growing family. The current Ashbridge house was built in 1853–54 by Jesse Ashbridge, and in 1899–1900 a second floor of bedrooms was added. Generations of Ashbridges have lived on the estate since 1894 and have carefully maintained the property. The house is a link to the area's early history, and archaeological excavations of the grounds have yielded artifacts dating back to Toronto's earliest history.

Around the turn of the 20th century, many prosperous Torontonians built their homes in the Beach area. It also became a popular vacation destination, so large and comfortable vacation accommodations were put up for holidayers who spent part of the summer there. However, the Depression and World War II meant that by the 1950s many of the fine old summer places had been converted to rooming houses. It is claimed that the area's resurgence began when young families discovered the Victorian charms of its housing stock, but some of that credit can be traced back to the results of a public meeting held one night in 1970 in the old Balmy Beach School on Beech Avenue. The city sent a demographer who pointed out that elderly people on small fixed incomes lived in homes on streets such as

Willow and Silverbirch, many of whom were converting part of their residences into rooming houses so they could afford to stay in them. The demographer told the audience that if a new school were built, young families would be attracted to the area. They would buy those old homes and return them to single-family residences to stabilize the neighbourhood. The audience bought his argument, the school was built, young families bought the old houses, and the renaissance was on.

Well-established institutions were also a stabilizing factor, and the area had several of those, including one of the oldest and best known: the Balmy Beach Club. It was called the Balmy Beach Lawn Bowling Club when it opened in 1905, and it quickly established a respected name in the world of athletics. Its walls are crowded with photographs of teams and individuals who triumphed locally, nationally, and internationally, while wearing the proud Old Gold and Royal Blue club colours.

It might be the healthy lifestyle engendered by all the sand and water, but the area spawned a surprising number of star athletes relative to its population. The Balmy Beach football team captured Grey Cups in 1927 and 1930, and the pre-war NHL star "Hooley" Smith as well as track stars Myrt Cook and Bobbie Rosenfeld, rowers Roy Nurse and Joe McNulty, and all-round athlete Ted Reeve were all born and bred in the east end. Amateur athletics were an expensive pursuit, but the club didn't benefit from liquor sales because it was officially "dry" until 1965, so weekly dances were a profitable and popular source of income. In 1939 the students at Malvern Collegiate decided to raise enough money to buy a fighter aircraft for the war effort, so they organized a series of dances at the club, and to save the expense of a live orchestra they played records over a portable sound system. The dances were steady money-makers and continued after the war — 10 cents a dance for a set of three, after which the floor was cleared to foil any freeloaders. They were held four nights a week and the Saturday night version featured live bands led by musicians such as George Hooey, Johnnie Minshull, and Jack Kent Cooke.

The Balmy Beach Club is situated at the southern end of Beech Avenue overlooking the eastern boardwalk that stretches almost two kilometres from Silver Birch Avenue to Coxwell Avenue. Sketchy city archives indicate that it has been around in one form or another since the 1880s or 1890s. At one time, a railing ran from the club to Hammersmith Avenue, but it was destroyed by a storm in the early 1950s that also demolished the tennis court at the Club. Until fairly recently, the boardwalk suffered from a built-in defect: it was below the Lake Ontario water level. Every spring large sections would be washed away by late winter storms that raised the lake level even higher. That problem was solved with an extensive restoration project that

Beach Metro News.

Not all the locals signed on when east end Toronto was given its official historical designation.

replaced wooden planks with ones that incorporated a recycled plastic composite (it lasted longer). Some residents accepted the change, but others felt the replacements just weren't as springy. The issue died down quickly, and while it may seem a trivial matter, it proves that it doesn't take much to inspire a controversy in the Beaches.

Or should that be the Beach? This is a question that has long inflamed passions of eastenders, especially in 1985 when street signs proclaiming the Beaches were installed along Queen Street. A violent uproar ensued. The signs came down two months later, and the matter has not been discussed in polite circles since.

But the Beachers didn't win all their battles. In 1987 residents were outraged when an attempt was made to cut down a 75-year-old maple tree on Queen Street to make way for a two-storey building with retail space. A 1500-name petition protesting the action was quickly gathered. When workmen came to cut down the maple, Heidi Lamporstofer, a nearby shop owner, and three others chained themselves to the massive trunk. Sadly, their efforts were to no avail. The tree came down, the building went up, and Queen Street continued its gradual change from a quiet local shopping area to a trendy district where the younger set browse in upscale retail outlets.

Tree huggers Richard and Heidi Lamperstorfer, Anne Mirlan, Reed Russell, and John Kervin.

Bennett Guinn, Ward 9 News.

Restaurants now share the strip with take-out operations like Enrico's Pizza — "You ring, we bring" — and though it left in 1988 similar operations have taken its place. Griffith's, a café run by Ron and Frances Aranas and their daughter Denise in the 1980s and 1990s successfully resisted this tide, though it could be argued that it prospered despite itself. Patrons entered the dining area through an archway bearing a Latin inscription, which translated means "Abandon hope all ye who enter here." This is a rather odd way to greet customers, but that was part of its eccentric charm. Service was spasmodic, the menu was solid but predictable, and the décor could be best described as early quixotic. My older daughter Judy and her husband Glenn Brodie were married at Griffith's on a beautiful day in May 1994. When the wedding pictures circulated a few weeks later people asked her why Christmas decorations were in the background if the wedding was held in the summer. All I can say by way of explanation is that if the Aranas family liked something they stuck with it.

Griffith's went out of business a few years later, but their Christmas spirit found an outlet in another local tradition. In 1990, two Queen Street merchants named Carol Nelson and Jean Simmons provided the funds for a tree-lighting ceremony to be held in Kew Park. The Beaches Lions Club took it over in 1994 and I have acted as master of ceremonies ever since. The lovely old park fills with young families, Santa Claus always arrives on schedule, and sometimes it even snows on cue.

In 1989 another event got its start in Kew Gardens and went on to attract an estimated 300,000 visitors — the Beaches Jazz Festival. Its early name was Streetfest and it began as a one-day event designed to showcase local talent. (As an aside, pianist Glenn Gould, film-maker Norman Jewison, and comedian John Candy grew up in the area and have all contributed to the area's reputation for entertainment.) An enthusiastic response expanded Streetfest to two days the following year. In 1991 American imports including Dewey Redman and

Glenn Gould house standing pianissimo.

Jerry Gonzalez and the Fort Apache Band performed on stage, and the following year musicians played on street corners over the course of three evenings. In 1993 it was renamed the Beaches International Jazz Festival with President Lido Chilelli and Artistic Director Bill King at the helm. The festival now runs for four days in the third week of July and attendance continues to grow, but so does controversy surrounding the annual event. Music lovers say there is very little real jazz (American acts in particular) at the Jazz Festival thanks to the higher cost of union rates paid in U.S. dollars. Neighbourhood groups complain about the impact of the big crowds and the noise and want the festival moved to nearby Woodbine Park. But Queen Street East merchants want those big crowds for big business.

Just south of the boardwalk and the park is another of the area's landmarks and one of the most-loved structures in the area — a homely little building on the water's edge called the Scarborough Beach Station, later renamed the Leuty Lifesaving Station. It was one of a string of similar facilities built along the waterfront in 1920. By 1993 it was declared to be structurally unsound and was in danger of being torn down until residents rallied to its aid. A Save Our Station committee was formed with former head lifeguard Chris Layton as chairman and funds for its restoration flowed in from T-shirt sales, harp concerts held in restaurants, and church raffle tickets for a mini version of the building

Gene Domagala.

This scale model of the Leuty Lifesaving Station, nicknamed "Little Leuty," was raffled off during the campaign to save the original structure.

John Bygh.

The station at the end of Leuty Avenue had its own life saved thanks to fundraising efforts by area residents.

nicknamed Little Leuty, which raised an additional
$5,000. The campaign raised $50,000 in all, and the
SOS Committee was presented with a Toronto Heritage
Board award for its efforts.

The company that built the Little Leuty free of
charge in 1995 also bought the land beneath the local
racetrack, an 83-acre complex bordered by Lakeshore
Boulevard to the south, Coxwell Avenue to the west,
Queen Street to the north, and Woodbine Avenue to
the east. The Woodbine track (changed its name to
Greenwood in 1963) ran its first Queen's Plate, named
for Queen Victoria, when Canada was only 16 years
old. (When the British Empire is ruled by a male it is
of course called the King's Plate.) The event had been
staged in various tracks around Ontario for 20 years
prior to that, but in 1883 the monarch decreed that it
never be held outside Toronto. In 1928 a double-deck
stand was added to the members' enclosure and
included a royal box from which King George and
Queen Elizabeth themselves watched the race in 1939.
They were the only reigning monarchs to see the race
in person. The last Plate race was held at the old Woodbine in 1955. The event is now held at the new
Woodbine track off Highway 27.

Woodbine was called the "streetcar track" because
the King and Queen routes brought bettors right to its
doors. The Red Rockets that shuttle faithfully from the
Harris Filtration plant all the way to Long Branch, a

90-minute journey that gives a view of everything that Toronto has to offer, are a fixture in the area. Residents have long been aware of the high-pitched squeal the streetcars produce when they negotiate the Neville Park loop. There are some who say it is the tortured cry of Ambrose Small, a Toronto businessman who disappeared many years ago after making a sizeable withdrawal from his bank. Others say it is the frustrated howl of motorists wondering where they can park their cars. This version is endorsed by a growing number of residents because as everyone knows there is nowhere to park in the Beach(es)!

The old Woodbine racetrack on Queen Street East broke bettors' hearts, and their wallets, for over three quarters of a century.

Charley the Gorilla kept crowds on their toes and proved a favourite with audiences for years.

IT'S A ZOO
OUT THERE

Scarborough

Scarborough was named by Elizabeth Graves Simcoe, the wife of Lieutenant Governor John Graves Simcoe, because she thought the cliffs facing Lake Ontario resembled the ones she remembered in Scarborough, England. The Canadian namesake was mostly farmland for many decades, and in 1939 the population was just 23,209. In 1950 that figure had doubled to 48,141, and by 1970 313,213 people lived in Scarborough. This jump was partly caused by a decision made by Reeve Oliver Crockford, who served from 1948 until 1955. During his tenure developers were allowed to build houses of smaller size than those permitted in surrounding municipalities, which helped spark a construction boom that continued for decades. That boom contributed to urban sprawl, which in turn led to Scarborough acquiring the ugly nickname Scarberia, a term that has bedevilled the area for years despite the efforts of politicians to forge a more inviting image.

Several years ago, police apprehended a man who was a suspect in a series of violent convenience store robberies in Scarborough. I happened to be in the vicinity so I was instructed to drop what I was doing and get some footage as he was led into the station. The suspect recognized me and engaged me in a lengthy conversation during the course of which he confessed that he was indeed guilty. The two officers who were taking the man in copied down every word and the man was quickly sentenced in court. I helped crack that case dammit, but people only remember me for those women.

In 1968 Toronto architect Raymond Moriyama was commissioned to create a structure that would provide an identity and focus for the people of Scarborough, and five years later, in 1973, the Scarborough Civic Centre opened its doors to the public. The nearby Scarborough Town Centre opened the same year and eventually government buildings and a light rail transit line connected the civic centre to the Kennedy subway station.

Peter Mykusz, City of Scarborough.

Longtime Scarborough mayor Gus Harris explains the symbols on the coat of arms to a curious reporter during City of the Future Week in 1985.

Developers and politicians wanted to jump-start Scarborough's growth, but that didn't fit the philosophy of long-time mayor Gus Harris, a homespun politician who liked the place just the way it was. He disdained the trappings of office and showed up at all functions in his own car, a battered old Buick with more than 150,000 miles on it. His elderly automobile was a source of embarrassment to his fellow politicians and various spin doctors who thought his style should better reflect

Scarborough's big-league ambitions. But old Gus must have struck a chord with the electorate because his popularity held fast until he announced his retirement November 30, 1988, after 37 years in elected office. His hold on the electorate was so firm that councilors with mayoral aspirations of their own often wondered despairingly which would stop running first, "Gus Harris or that damn rusty old car of his."

The Scarberia image was used to great comic effect by famous Scarborough native Mike Myers, who based *Wayne's World*, a hilarious send-up on his youth there. Myers has gone on to bigger triumphs over the years, particularly as his cinematic creation Austin Powers. Although he doesn't get back to Toronto much, he has never lost affection for his hometown. In fact, several years ago he drew up a list of the four things he missed most about Toronto: Cherry Blossom candy; ketchup-flavoured potato chips; a six-pack of Molson Canadian beer, known fondly as a Scarborough suitcase; and me. The next time he returned to Toronto we had an emotional reunion on the steps of the Legislature at Queen's Park. CFTO brought me out of retirement so the event could be recorded for posterity.

Another famous Wayne, the NHL's greatest scorer, came to Toronto very early in his career as a professional hockey player. Every Canadian knew of his goal-scoring exploits in the lower ranks of the game, but a considerable number of self-styled hockey experts believed he

— Ken Kerr, SUN

BUSSING BUDDIES ... CFTO's Glenn Cochrane holds a bundle of Mike Myers' favorite goodies when the two got together at Queen's Park yesterday for a spot on the TV station.

Beer and chips?
Party on, Mike

Ken Kerr, Toronto Sun.

By TRISH TERVIT
Toronto Sun

What, no Grey Poupon?

It wasn't mustard Canadian actor Mike Myers was craving during his visit home to Toronto yesterday, but a frosty cool one.

In town to promote his new movie, *Austin Powers: International Man of Mystery*, Myers was presented a few of his favorite Canadian things by his own idol, the legendary CFTO reporter Glenn Cochrane.

Bags of ketchup-flavored potato chips and boxes of Lowney's Cherry Blossom candy were lavished on the star, much to his delight.

"You don't get ketchup chips down there. The first thing I do when I get off the plane is call my mom and they get some," quipped the star of *Wayne's World* and *Saturday Night Live.*

And the candy, "they sell it on the black market" in Los Angeles.

Perhaps most welcome were the two "Scarboro suitcases" Cochrane gave him — six-packs of Molson Canadian and Labatt's Blue.

Ironically Myers' hair closely resembled Cochrane's thick crop — "I'm sporting a Cochrane!" Myers joked.

Not!

Mike Myers and I share a tender moment during a visit Scarborough's favourite son made to his home town.

would be quickly driven out of the pros because of the much rougher calibre of play at the elite level. As a result, the press conference held to promote an ice cream bar named for Gretzky was poorly attended despite the availability of all the free ice cream you could eat. If only I had asked him to autograph the wrappers I could now be vacationing on the Riviera.

Beyond "Wayne's World" is that sprawling, fascinating, and ever-evolving kingdom known as the Toronto Zoo. The zoo provided an endless source of stories for me, but getting to those stories was an arduous experience due to a policy established by the late Tommy Thompson when he was the zoo's general director. A recital of Tommy's many qualities would be incomplete without mentioning that he cherished the trappings of office, including a golf cart kept on standby lest he needed it to whirr off to settle a problem at the llama paddock. When he was away it was securely locked up until his return.

The zoo is on a 700-acre site that is fully exposed to the blistering heat of summer and the chilly blasts of winter, so getting around the grounds on foot posed something of a problem. To make matters worse, cameras had a lot of ancillary equipment, including a tripod the size of a redwood tree. Even so Tommy didn't make his vehicle available to the news crews. It was a mark of the affection the media had for him that nobody complained. Tommy had been a well-known and popular

Tommy Thompson (with the loudspeaker) shares survival tips with King Clancy and Harold Ballard while zoo boss Ron Barbaro looks on.

figure in Toronto for some time, but he gained international attention during his tenure as Toronto Parks Commissioner when he posted PLEASE WALK ON THE GRASS signs in all of the city's parkland. He was possessed of great personal charm and a keen appreciation of the value of well-maintained public grounds. His appointment as the zoo's boss in April of 1978 was met with widespread approval.

Toby Styles, senior keeper at the zoo and later public relations manager, was equally popular. I remember being in a pasture with him one warm summer day when he coaxed a moose over to where we were standing. A stout wire fence separated us, which I found a comfort because while it was a gentle moose it was also a very large one. But if Toby talked to animals, he also talked to the press.

One Labour Day, an orangutan fell into a pond in its enclosure while chasing after some food and immediately got into difficulty. An onlooker scaled the security fence and began giving the poor creature mouth-to-mouth resuscitation and it wasn't long before a huge crowd gathered to watch the drama. Patrick McCarthy was working in the zoo's public relations department and when he passed the news along to his boss Toby's first words were "Tell the press." The unfortunate primate died the next day, but we got the story and it was a good one.

Many of the best stories about the zoo featured the

great apes, and one of my favourites was Charley the gorilla. Charley was big even for a gorilla. He used to sit all day with his arms folded across his chest while he chewed on a piece of straw. He never took his eyes off the audience, but when Charley figured the crowd was large enough he would rush over and smack the glass with his right paw, startling the crowd, only to return to his post and wait for the next mob of unsuspecting onlookers to show up. When he was at the top of his glass-thumping form old Charley put on the best show in town.

I believed Charley acted out because he was bored, something Dave Barney, manager of animal care at the zoo, says is not good for his health. Animals in the wild spend 14 to 18 hours a day looking for food, but a zoo is able to feed most of them everything they need in less than half an hour. Staff, therefore, have to maintain the health of the animals *and* keep them interested in their habitat. At one time, zoo animals were kept in dirt surroundings because zoologists believed this duplicated their natural environment, but it was found that parasites developed in the soil, killing the animals. Officials then switched to concrete enclosures (those who visited the old Riverdale Zoo in Toronto will remember what a depressing sight that was). Modern zoos now use artificial dirt similar to potting soil that has good draining qualities. This soil is placed over a concrete bed and at periodic intervals the soil is simply scraped off the concrete and replaced with a fresh supply.

Dave and his department have also focused on ways to keep the creatures curious about their surroundings. "We don't teach them tricks," he says, "we teach them behaviour enrichment." This approach takes some interesting forms. For instance, a log made in the zoo's huge workshop has several hidden holes that handlers tuck food into. The apes smell the food, but because it is difficult to get at, they use a stick to poke at the log, keeping both the animal busy and zoo-goers entertained.

It isn't just the animals that act wild, however. Some of the staff veterans still speak of the woman who was found throwing barbequed chicken to the lions. Before being escorted off the premises she told staff she had permission to feed the lions from Pierre Trudeau and Queen Victoria. Then there was the man who jogged through the gemsbok enclosure with his birth certificate in his mouth. With stuff like that going on how can the animals possibly be bored?

One bitterly cold winter day I went to the zoo with cameraman John Rygh to see how the polar bears were getting along in the sub-zero weather. In the summer the bears' enclosure featured a sunken pool, but due to frigid temperatures the water had frozen and expanded. When one of the bears stood on the ice, reared up to its full height, it was eye-to-eye with John, sticking its nose right into the camera lens. Things didn't look good for John, especially when the bear opened its mouth, but he stood his ground and got the shot. That was the kind of dedication shown by every cameraperson I worked with at CFTO.

Scarborough is still considered an emerging part of the City of Toronto, but it is also the repository of many important reminders of the city's history. The post-war building frenzy led to the destruction of many landmark buildings in the heart of downtown Toronto. For the most part the demolished structures ended up as rubble in landfill sites. But parts of those edifices are still on view thanks to a man named Spencer Clark. Clark and his wife Rosa started the Guild of All Arts in 1932. The purpose of the Guild was to provide working space for artists in several different disciplines, and in later years it was known as the dignified Guild Inn.

Clark realized that a significant part of Toronto's architectural heritage was being lost in the dust and noise of the downtown renovation and he embarked on a rescue mission that saved remnants of 60 buildings, which are on view to this day on the spacious grounds of the old Guild Inn. A set of stone carvings remains from the *Globe and Mail* building, which was demolished in 1974 to make way for First Canadian Place. There are also pieces of the white marble façade of the Imperial Bank of Canada, which stood on a site now occupied by the Canadian Imperial Bank of Commerce at 2 Bloor Street West. A stone lion is a reminder of the O'Keefe Brewery at Victoria and Gould streets, which

The Bank of Toronto façade was the setting for a production of A Funny Thing Happened on the Way to the Forum.

This remnant from an old downtown Toronto building is one of many on the Old Guild Inn grounds overlooking Lake Ontario.

now is a part of Ryerson College. Near the lion is an Ionic column from the Registry of Deeds and Land Titles, which once stood in all its Greek Revival glory on a site now used for underground parking at City Hall. Admission to the Guild Inn is free and the voyage of discovery begins at the entrance gates to the grounds, gates that once stood at Stanley Barracks. Thanks to the foresight of Spencer and Rosa Clark, an important part of Toronto's past has been preserved for generations to come.

SIGNING OFF FOR THE LAST TIME

Glenn Cochrane, recipient of a City of Toronto citation honoring his many years on CFTO-TV, receives a kiss from Councillor Kay Gardner, reminiscent of the way he used to end his reports.

Glenn Cochrane takes final bow after 22 years of making us laugh

By Jim Wilkes
TORONTO STAR

He's got a great face for radio.

But Glenn Cochrane has been a fixture on local television for 22 years, beamed into living rooms across southern Ontario by CFTO-TV.

Today it all ends.

Cochrane is retiring from the station two months before he turns 65 to try his hand at teaching, volunteer work and just plain relaxing.

"It's psychologically important for me to quit before I have to," he said yesterday before receiving a citation from the City of Toronto in one of the busiest weeks of a very busy career.

Metro Chairman Alan Tonks proclaimed it Glenn Cochrane Week in Metro and the diminutive reporter has been shuttled all over town to collect awards and accolades.

He was paraded before North York council on Wednesday in Mayor Mel Lastman's

trademark black-and-white-striped Bad Boy outfit.

The Scarborough fire department made him an honorary chief and chauffeured him to a council meeting in one of its big pumpers.

Yesterday, the TTC thought of a better way to get him to city hall. It renamed a streetcar the Glenn Cochrane Special and gave him his own inspector's cap.

Just the wacky kind of stuff he's often covered as CFTO's feature and community reporter.

"There's a greater premium placed on bad news than there is on good news," he said. "In TV, the phrase is, 'If it bleeds, it leads.'

"I made people laugh."

In a business where news anchors and reporters come and go on the whims of fashion or the onset of wrinkles, Cochrane has become a media star despite his rumpled suits, glasses and spud-like nose.

Maybe it was all those women with

whom he used to surround himself, before such things became politically incorrect.

For many years it was his on-air signature. Young women, old women, married women, single women, all helping him illustrate the story. Invariably, he'd get a kiss on the cheek to close the piece.

He was all business when he started in 1961 as a reporter for the Hamilton Spectator. He was also an editor for the Canadian Press wire service before he decided there was a better future for him in television than print journalism.

He started at CFTO as a writer in 1969 and it was three years before he went in front of the cameras.

Celebrity has its perks. He was a stretcher bearer during a performance of The Nutcracker and was once voted Toronto's Most Lovable Guy.

But his bottom line is simple.

"Just bringing attention to ordinary people," he said.

"That's my greatest pleasure."

The end of an era.

I stepped astride this camel during a 1999 campaign to raise funds for senior's residences in Toronto.

A triumphant moment during a Star Wars promotion.

BIBLIOGRAPHY

BOOKS AND REPORTS

Benn, Carl. *Historic Fort York*. Toronto: Natural Heritage/
Natural History, 1993.

Canadian Cancer Society, Ontario Division. *Very Special
People: The Achievement of the Canadian Cancer Society in
Ontario*. Toronto: ccs Ontario Division, 1984.

Caulfield, Jon. *The Tiny Perfect Mayor: David Crombie and
Toronto's Reform Aldermen*. Toronto: James Lorimer & Co,
Publishers, 1974.

Cochrane, Jean. *Kensington*. Toronto: Boston Mills Press,
2002.

Corelli, Rae. *The Toronto That Used to Be*. Toronto: Toronto
Star Limited, 1964.

Crombie, David. *Yonge Street, Lakeshore Blvd, Parliament
Street and the Waterfront: Criteria, Constraints and
Considerations for Redevelopment*. Toronto: Toronto
Executive Committee, 1974.

Donegan, Rosemary. *Spadina Avenue*. Vancouver: Douglas &
McIntyre, 1985.

Fulford, Robert. *Accidental City: The Transformation of
Toronto*. Toronto: MacFarlane, Walter & Ross, 1995.

Gittins, Susan. *CTV The Television Wars*. Toronto: Stoddart
Publishing Co., 1999.

Gould, Allan. *The Toronto Book.* Toronto: Key Porter
Books, 1983.
Guild Inn. *The Spencer Clark Collection of Historic
Architecture at the Guild Inn.* Scarborough: The Guild
Inn, 1980.
Heritage Toronto with Draper Street Reference Group.
Draper Street Heritage Conservation District Study.
Toronto: Heritage Toronto, 1998.
Lidgold, Carole M. *The History of the Guild Inn.*
Scarborough: Brookbridge Publishing House, 2000.
Lorimer, James. *The Ex: A Picture History of the Canadian
National Exhibition.* Toronto: James Lewis & Samuel,
Publishers, 1973.
Mirvish, Ed. *Honest Ed Mirvish: How to Build an Empire
on an Orange Crate or 121 Lessons I Never Learned in
School.* Toronto: Key Porter Books, 1993.
Nash, Knowlton. *The Swashbucklers: The Story of Canada's
Battling Broadcasters.* Toronto: McClelland & Stewart,
2001.
Sewell, John. *The Shape of the City.* Toronto: University of
Toronto Press, 1993.
Spelt, Jacob. *Toronto: Canadian Cities Series.* Toronto:
Collier-Macmillan Canada, 1973.
Taylor, Rachel. *A Common Thread: A History of Toronto's
Garment Industry.* Toronto: Beth Tzedec Reuben and
Helene Dennis Museum, 2003.
Toronto City Council. *City of Toronto Municipal Handbook.*
Toronto: City of Toronto, 1971.

NEWSPAPERS

Alden Baker, "Sewell Loses Bid for Re-election," *Globe and Mail*, 11 November 1980.

Brian Hogan, "Alex," *Toronto Telegram*, 14 February 1963.

"Building Limit Called Insane," *Toronto Star*, 1 March 1975.

"City Approves New Controls," *Toronto Star*, 21 February 1975.

Claire Hoy, "Decision 'Most Agonizing' for Cabinet, Davis Says," *Toronto Star*, 4 June 1975.

Debra Black, "Just Call Them Dr. Mirvish," *Toronto Star*, 12 June 2004.

Edward Clifford, "Honest Ed Buys Royal Alex," *Globe and Mail*, 16 February 1963.

"End Expressway at Eglinton Liberal Urges," *Toronto Star*, 4 June 1975.

Ernest Rawley, "The Alex," *Toronto Telegram*, 8 August 1961.

"Festival's Charity Felt Year-round," *National Post*, 2 August 2003.

Frank Jones, "Stop-and-Go: History of the Spadina Expressway," *Toronto Star*, 4 June 1975.

Herbert Whittaker, "Show Business: Owner of Alex Plans Party," *Globe and Mail*, 13 August 1963.

Jessie McCarron, "Royal Alex: Red Carpet Treatment," *Toronto Telegram*, 13 August 1963.

Jim Coyle, "Recalling a True Giant Among City's Builders," *Toronto Star*, 22 June 2004.

Jim Wilkes, "Danforth Awash in Music and Costumes," *Toronto Star*, 24 March 2003.

John Sewell, "Medicine for What is Ailing Toronto," *Toronto Star*, 5 October 1980.

Liane Heller, "High Profile David Garrick," *Toronto Star*, 4 March 1984.

"Liberals Endorse Halt to Spadina Freeway," *Toronto Star*, 2 June 1975.

Loren Lind, "Aldermanic Ups and Downs in Great Zoning Debate," *Toronto Star*, 2 February 1978.

Martin Knelman, "To Let: Planetarium, Must Share," *Toronto Star*, 18 April 2004.

Mary Nersesdian, "Danforth Comes Alive," *Toronto Star*, 8 August 2003.

Michael Best, "Transit Plans Awry in Wake of Decision," *Toronto Star*, 4 June 1975.

Nathan Cohen, "The Royal Alex Begins a New Year," *Toronto Star*, 7 September 1963.

Nathan Cohen, "The Royal Alex Saved," *Toronto Star*, 13 February 1963.

Nicholas Keung, and Philip Mascoll, "Caravan Nearing End of Its Road," *Toronto Star*, 22 March 2004.

Norm McCabe, "He Fought City Hall and Won," *Toronto Star*, 4 June 1975.

"Not Looking for a Profit," *Toronto Star*, 16 February 1963.

Paul Dalby, "Caravan Imports Cod," *Toronto Star*, 21 June 1975.

Richard Griffin, "Jays are Proud to be Reaching Out to Gay Community," *Toronto Star*, 25 June 2004.

"Royal Alex Sale Expected Next Week," *Globe and Mail*, 13 February 1963.

Scott Young, "Royal Alex," *Globe and Mail*, 19 June 1963.

"Spadina Halt Delays Permanent Mall," *Toronto Star*, 2 June 1975.

"The Spadina Decision: Right Philosophy, Questionably Applied," *Toronto Star*, 4 June 1975.

"This is a Non-Growth Policy," *Toronto Star*, 12 August 1974.

Warren Gerrard, and Val Sears, "Will it Choke Growth or Improve City?" *Toronto Star*.

Zena Cherry, "Parade of Daffodils," *Globe and Mail*, 1 April 1982.

MAGAZINES

John Bugailiskis, and Lesley Young, "CHIN Celebrates 30 Years," *Broadcaster*, Vol. 55, No. 9, October 1996, p. 14.

Robert Lewis, "The Greening of Toronto," *Time*, 23 June 1975, pp. 8–17.

Michael J. Rudman, "The History of These Graves," *The York Pioneer*, Vol. 94, 1999, pp. 17–28.

ACKNOWLEDGEMENTS

I do not know why some consider the act of writing a book to be a lonely pursuit. During the course of my labours many people provided enormous help. I thank the following people and institutions who smoothed the path with their willing and knowledgeable assistance: Dave Barney, Ken Bingham, Marilyn Brooks, Jim Carmichael, Linda Cobon, Jean Cochrane, David Crombie, Linda Dixon, Gene Domagala, Gwen Egan, Alfred Fulton, Aurelio Galipo, David Garrick, Joy Gugeler, Joice Guspie, Zena Kossar, Olive Koyama, Russell Lazar, the Lombardi family, Paul Magder, Patrick McCarthy, David Mirvish, Tonia Mykolyshyn, Walter Oster, David Rotman, Chao Tam; and the staff of the Urban Affairs, Toronto Reference, Beaches, Pape, and Riverdale libraries as well as the City of Toronto Archives.